400TH ANNIVERSARY OF KING JAMES'S SCHOOL IN ALMONDBURY

1608 - 2008

King James presents a Charter to his Schole in Allmonbury.

KING JAMES'S SCHOOL
IN ALMONDBURY

AN ILLUSTRATED HISTORY
1608 - 2008

KING JAMES'S SCHOOL IN ALMONDBURY

AN ILLUSTRATED HISTORY
1608 - 2008

Edited by

ROGER DOWLING
JOHN A HARGREAVES

THE OLD ALMONDBURIANS' SOCIETY • KING JAMES'S SCHOOL • ALMONDBURY

Frontispiece:
James I and VI
by John de Critz (1604)
reproduced by permission of
National Galleries of Scotland

Photograph of Charter by courtesy of
West Yorkshire Archive Service

Front flyleaf drawing
by Bradley S Shaw
(Art Master
King James's Grammar School
1903 - 1920)

Drawing on page 99 by The Very Reverend
William Foxley Norris, Governor of
King James's Grammar School (1889-1901)
and Dean of Westminster (1925-1937)

Typeset in Perpetua and Gill Sans
Design: Roger Dowling
Print: Hart & Clough Print Group
Ezra House, West 26 Business Park,
Cleckheaton BD19 4TQ

Published by
The Old Almondburians' Society
King James's School
Almondbury
Huddersfield HD4 6SG
www.oas.org.uk

Sponsored by the
King James's School Foundation

ISBN 978 0 9557314 0 2

Contents

FOREWORD

I WAS THERE on that sunny day in 1958 when the Countess of Scarborough opened the new cricket pavilion. In fact, I still have a programme!

With advancing years it is sometimes frightening to realise that one has lived through and experienced events that are currently studied as history. Certainly, the fifty years since the 350th anniversary have seen the arrival of The Beatles, the death of John F Kennedy, the landing on the moon, the end of the Cold War, the fall of communism, and the advent of the world wide web – not to mention the admission of girls to King James's School.

Our School, adapting to changes like a chameleon, has, through the good offices of many men and women, remained a rock throughout; always there to be remembered, consulted, cherished and visited by Almondburians of every generation. Its connection with, and contribution to, the development of local and national history has always been a source of inspiration to pupils, parents, teachers and the wider community.

The Old Almondburians' Society as we know it today was formed as a result of a meeting convened by Taylor Dyson with a few old scholars on 17th March 1920. Since then the Society has continued to maintain its aims of upholding the honour and status of the School and providing members a means of contacting each other and maintaining links with the School. The Society is grateful for the efforts of countless committee members who have given freely of their time in ensuring its success over the years. As I write these words the executive committee is busy organising the 400th Anniversary Dinner to be held on 22nd November 2008 and the Anniversary steering group is coordinating a wide range of events to ensure a weekend to remember.

We hope you will enjoy reading this fascinating account of the School's past 400 years, generously sponsored by the King James's School Foundation which will enable a souvenir copy to be presented to each pupil at the School. This publication is just one of a number of special commemorative items, all of which are available on-line on our website (www.oas.org.uk) or from the School. Contact with members and availability of information is now considerably enhanced with our web presence and the Society looks forward to a continual expansion in membership up to its own centenary in 2020 – the next milestone!

My friend and contemporary Richard Taylor and I are proud to be Joint Chairmen at this time and wish the School and the Society well for the future.

Floreat Schola Almondburiensis!

Paul Balderstone (1954-1962)
The Old Almondburians' Society

ACKNOWLEDGEMENTS

A YEAR AGO, when I was updating the website of The Old Almondburians' Society, I needed a page about the history of the School. Accordingly, I contacted Gerald Hinchliffe, author of the excellent *History of King James's School in Almondbury* and a notable Old Almondburian himself, and asked him if he would mind writing a few hundred words for the page I had in mind.

With the benefit of hindsight it was an astonishingly naïve request to ask anyone – even the redoubtable Gerald – to condense the history of the School since 1608 into just 'a few hundred words'. When I asked a couple of months later how the task was proceeding, Gerald reported the good news that he had finished the first 2,000 words. The bad news was that he had only got as far as 1695.

Then Providence took a hand with my involvement in the present publication. When it was decided to produce an 'Illustrated History of King James's School' to mark the 400th anniversary of its Royal Charter, who was better placed than Gerald to provide a major literary input? And so it was that the 'few hundred words' became, at the end of the day, the 18,000 words that form the backbone of this publication. Gratitude is an inadequate word with which to record my appreciation to Gerald for his outstanding contribution.

My sincere thanks too to all the other contributors who so willingly put their daily tasks to one side in order to meet what were no doubt entirely unreasonable publication deadlines. Their personal recollections of their time at King James's will, I am sure, bring to life what might otherwise have been merely a dry historical account of events that occurred many years ago.

The original inspired idea of producing this book came from my fellow-editor John Hargreaves, Head of History at King James's from 1979 to 1990. I must record my thanks to him for all his input as the project has progressed.

Thanks are also due to Nicky Green, Walter Raleigh and their colleagues at the School for so patiently dealing with the many telephone calls and queries that a task of this nature inevitably involves. Pat Reid, now retired but performing a vital service in 'sorting out the archives', was a tremendous help in locating suitable early photographs and cuttings, and I am also similarly indebted to Jenny Ainger in the School library. The King James's School 400 Committee, for whom the book was just one of many initiatives to mark the 400th anniversary, was a source of ongoing support and encouragement. Many Old Almondburians – far too numerous to mention by name – provided personal recollections for which I am deeply grateful.

Outside the School, I should like to thank the King James's School Foundation, Yorkshire Archaeological Society, West Yorkshire Archive Service, the *Huddersfield Examiner*, and Almondbury Parish Church. Jonathan Webb at Webb Aviation took the superb aerial photographs of the School and perceptive proof-reading was undertaken by Keith Crawshaw and Mark Dowling.

Finally, I must thank Martyn Hicks at Screenprint Productions Limited and Alan Hirst at printers Hart & Clough, without whose expert help at the production stage this book would, quite simply, never have seen light of day.

Roger Dowling, Lymm
November 2007

INTRODUCTION

KING JAMES'S SCHOOL IN ALMONDBURY is the oldest school in Kirklees and one of the most historic schools in Yorkshire. Indeed few comprehensive schools anywhere in the country can claim a virtually continuous history on a single site, which is well documented from the middle of the sixteenth century. Moreover, few schools can boast such a thriving association of former students and staff which supports the continuing development of the school in so many ways, including the sponsorship of this new illustrated history of the school to mark the four hundredth anniversary in 2008 of the granting of the royal charter to the school in 1608.

A variety of contributors have been assembled to provide this survey of the school's fascinating history over a period of half a millennium. **Gerald Hinchliffe** traces the fascinating history of the School from the Reformation, through the English Civil Wars, the Industrial Revolution and the two World Wars of the twentieth century. **Dave Bush**, whose arrival at the school in 1961 was recorded in Hinchliffe's history and who served on the staff until his retirement in 1996, then provides a personal perspective on the history of the school during its transformation from a grammar into an 11-16 comprehensive school, drawing upon a rich store of amusing anecdotes.

Richard and Andrew Taylor contribute an affectionate and perceptive portrait of their father's influential and inspirational headship, while **Graham Cliffe**, one of a number of Almondburians who have followed successful legal careers, recounts the campaign to ensure that historic endowments were employed for the benefit of the school.

For Taylor Dyson, the author of the very first history of King James's School published in 1926, history was not so much a succession of distant facts but rather an exploration of how the past has helped to shape the world in which we live today. **Robert Lamb**, the current head teacher, in an informative account of recent developments at the School and its aspirations for the future, links the School's achievement of specialist science status in 2004 with its emergence as a pioneering centre of scientific excellence in the Victorian era.

Harry Taylor once famously turned Henry Ford's debunking dismissal of history on its head when he declared that history was 'the Bunk' at Almondbury and appropriately **Roger Dowling** traces the evolution of the school's distinctive built environment. He also makes a personal selection of some Old Almondburians who have gained wider public recognition.

The distinguished social historian of modern Britain **Edward Royle**, whose success in achieving an open exhibition to read history at Cambridge in 1961 was also recorded in Hinchliffe's history, concludes by relating the history of the School to its wider historical context.

Taylor Dyson and his successors have recognised the influence of history in developing the shared values and traditions which have helped shape the distinctive character and sense of community still embodied by King James's School today and which will provide the springboard for its future development.

John A Hargreaves, Halifax
November 2007

● *John Hargreaves taught at King James's School from 1971-90 and was Head of Religious Education from 1974-80 and Head of History from 1979-90. He also served as librarian of the Taylor Dyson local history collection. From 1990-2006 he taught at Batley Girls' High School serving as Head of History and Head of Humanities and is currently Research Fellow in History at the University of Huddersfield. He published a history of Halifax in 1999 and is now working on a new history of Huddersfield.*

The Free Grammar Schole of Kinge James in Almonbury

GERALD HINCHLIFFE tells the story of the School's precarious early days and its growth over the centuries to become a notable Yorkshire grammar school

O WORTHY ALMONDBURIAN, look at the photograph (left) taken from the tower of Almondbury Church and you will gaze upon more than four hundred years of your School's history. Each one of you has been an important part of that history.

Each one of you will have memories of those days long ago when you hurried down St Helen's Gate in pursuit of knowledge (or maybe as Shakespeare put it, 'creeping like snail unwillingly to school'!). St Helen's Gate, Arkenley, the Farnley Valley all lie before you. Into your thoughts come incidents, high drama, friends, and brilliant or eccentric pedagogues. They are of your time, and also of earlier times from the evidence which our forbears have left behind. They are so much a part of us, so vivid a reminder of what was once a way of life.

Before the Charter: the 'chapell of old tyme'

Although the story of the charter begins in 1608, the history of the School is, in fact, even older. If you look at the photograph, you will see, in the middle distance, a house with two upstairs windows. That is Kirk Royd, half way down St Helen's Gate. It is the site of a chantry chapel, almost certainly the chapel of St Helena. It was common in the early fifteenth century for such chapels to be erected wherein a priest could pray for the souls of departed gentry. The priest in many cases combined this role with teaching boys Latin. Latin was in those days a spoken language in many professions and activities, and notably in church services. The priest would prepare boys for their choral role and for reading the bible. Invariably they were the sons of local well-to-do gentry.

St Helena was the patron saint of the Kayes of Woodsome and it is generally assumed that the chapel was founded around 1400 by an early John Kaye in memory of his father, William. This chapel and many other chantry chapels were at risk once Henry VIII broke with Rome, and sought to dissolve monasteries and other religious houses and to confiscate their revenues and endowments.

Thus he and I dyd shifte yt

John Kaye of Woodsome (1530-1594) kept a diary (a 'Commonplace Book'), full of human interest. Above all, he made one entry which ranks in significance with the granting of the Charter by King James in 1608. It reads:

Where his Auncesters buyldid a chapell of old tyme in the lone end above ye Butts at St Elynvell about prmo Edw.. sexti. He and I dyd shifte yt and by concent of the parishe dyd translate the same into the Scole howsse that now is. And I dyd p'cure one Mr Smyth a good scolar to com and teach Here.

In the first year of Edward VI's reign (1547) John and his father, Arthur, had the chapel dismantled and rebuilt roughly on the site of the present Schoolhouse. We must regard John as a worthy fellow Almondburian. He and

---

Gerald Hinchliffe is well known to most Old Almondburians as the author of *A History of King James's Grammar School in Almondbury*. He attended the School from 1933 to 1940 and then went to the University of Leeds where he graduated with an Honours degree in English in 1943. Between 1943 and 1946 he served in the Duke of Wellington's Regiment and on demobilisation he returned to the University for another year. He then joined the staff of the Scarborough Boys' High School where he remained until 1955. During this time he did research work in education and received the degree of Master of Education in 1955. In that year he was appointed to the University of Nottingham where he subsequently became Senior Lecturer in Education. He retired in 1987.

his wife married at the age of 15, and they had fifteen children of whom a few went up to Cambridge. He managed a large estate, and he found time to write poetry. What a man!

Of Mr Smyth we know little, but we do have a record of one schoolmaster at the School, a certain Richard Hurst.

Richard Hurst (1563)

The School in Hurst's time probably had just a handful of pupils. Hurst taught them Latin and catechised them in the mother tongue. He was not a graduate, but he had probably been a scholar at some Yorkshire grammar school. It is tempting to speculate that he had been a pupil at the 'chapel of old tyme'!

Who were his pupils? In 1969 Harry Taylor, the distinguished Headmaster of King James's at that time, transcribed the parish registers and came across an entry dated 9th September 1564. It recorded a marriage, indicated the witnesses, and then in conclusion came this detail:

… his quoque scolasticis Thoma Beaumont Edwardo Nettleton Roberto Kaye filio Egidii Carole Kaye cum aliis.

These are undoubtedly the first named Almondburians. For the benefit of those who were not privileged to have been taught by such classical scholars and true Almondburians as Jim Toomey or Dave Bush, here is a translation:

… and also with these scholars Thomas Beaumont, Edward Nettleton, Robert

Kaye, son of Giles, Charles Kaye with others.

These scholars bear illustrious Almondbury names. Robert Kaye, son of Giles, was to die at the age of 23 and to leave the School a valuable legacy. Thomas Beaumont, 45 years later, was to bring the Royal Charter to Almondbury. The Nettleton family were to endow both School and town. Charles is almost certainly son of John Kaye of Woodsome.

The Royal Charter

By the year 1608, the School lay empty, derelict and 'destitute of teaching.' Certain gentlemen were prepared to endow a new school; all that was needed was a royal charter ('letters patent') to ensure the permanence and prestige of the school.

So it was that our Thomas Beaumont, old Almondburian, went to London with a petition in the hope of securing the King's favour. He also had family legal matters to resolve and took many months to complete his mission. However, one day he wrote to a relative:

I have gotten the patent for Almondbury free school under seal which I might make an errand to bring down …

Impecunious and weary, he returned and thus a new chapter – and a royal name – began.

The man who started it all: John Kaye of Woodsome

WOODSOME HALL stands just over half a mile from King James's School and its fortunes over the centuries have been linked inextricably with those of its neighbour. In 1547 it was occupied by Arthur Kaye and his wife Beatrix. Henry VIII had, a few years earlier, broken with the church of Rome and had set into motion the dissolution of the monasteries.

Then, in 1545, a further Act was passed giving the King power to seize the chantries – chapels endowed to celebrate masses for the souls of their donors. Such a chantry,

known as St Helen's Chapel, was located just above in St Helen's Gate, a few hundred yards up the hill; it had been set up centuries before by the Kayes' ancestors. The chapel had a dual role: it also provided valuable education for the local children. The Kayes therefore decided that urgent action was required.

And so it was that the 19-year-old John Kaye, with the help of his father, set about the task of pulling down the chapel stone by stone and reconstructing it on the site of the present School. The task accomplished, they appointed 'one Mr Smyth, a good scolar' to come and teach there.

The chantry may have gone, but John Kaye's timely action had saved the day. Little did he know what history he had set into motion.

If you look at the Charter, admire its beauty and absorb all its provisions (!), you will realise the size of the project which confronted the 'six honest men' who now had the responsibility for creating a school free from the insecurities of the past – Robert Kaye of Woodsome; William Ramsden of Longley; George Crossland, vicar of Almondbury; Nicholas Fenay of Fenay; Richard Appleyard of Over Longley; and Robert Nettleton of Almondbury. The first task was to build a Schoolhouse.

Early days

What remained of the derelict building which the Kayes had erected was pulled down and a new Schoolhouse was built. This took three years and it opened its doors in 1611. It is probable that the first Master was a certain Nicholas Greaves, since he was definitely in residence by 1619. A Cambridge graduate, he was at Almondbury until 1640. He had only a few pupils. In modern terms, it was a primary/secondary school, with pupils travelling to the School from various parts of the parish.

Greaves seems to have been a good teacher and a number of his pupils went up to Cambridge. Mathias Crossland went to Christ's College and graduated in 1620. Others – like Richard Sykes of Kirkheaton and William Horsfall of Storthes Hall – followed; the latter subsequently became a Governor of the School. It is likely also that his brother Richard, who fought for the Royalist cause at Marston Moor, was also a pupil. You may wonder how long these pupils attended the School and what they were taught. When George Edward Dodson was awarded the Dartmouth Medal in 1854 he was described as being the

longest serving boy to have attended the School. He had been there six years; in Greaves' time, four years would have been the maximum.

What were they taught? It was expected that pupils had the basic skills on entry. Thereafter the curriculum was strongly classical. Formidable studies! How many of you would have survived to meet the demands to write some Latin verse or prose, translate Cicero or Vergil (all before lunch!), and follow it with an afternoon of Greek grammar? And no five-day week: Saturday was for the catechism and polishing the basic skills.

After dispensing this academic diet for some 25 years, Greaves left and was succeeded by George Farrand. However, within a year Charles I had raised his standard at Nottingham and everyone, including Farrand and his pupils, was embroiled in one way or another in Civil War.

Despite the Royalist allegiance of the Kayes, Ramsdens, Horsfalls, Fenays and Beaumonts, Almondbury became a rallying point for the Roundhead cause. The handful of boys heading down St Helen's Gate must have encountered many a Roundhead soldier, and the latter's roistering in the alehouses was not uncommon.

George Farrand was a Royalist and did not hesitate to proclaim his allegiance. Never a day passed without prayers being said for the King and his restoration was duly celebrated. Farrand survived and ruled the School for 40 years. A man of principle, a poet, a compassionate cleric, he made his mark.

A succession of Masters followed. There were several

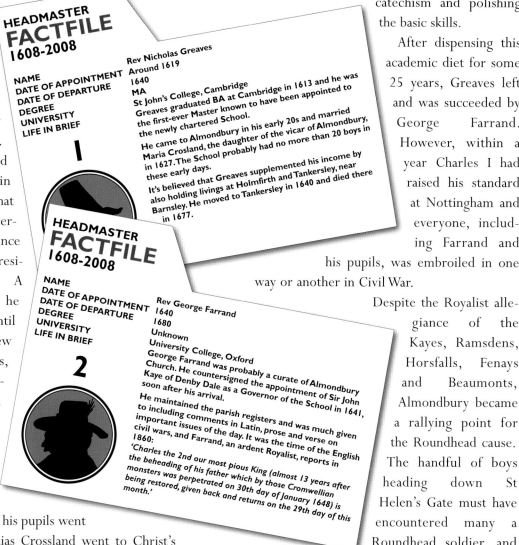

HEADMASTER FACTFILE 1608-2008

1

NAME Rev Nicholas Greaves
DATE OF APPOINTMENT Around 1619
DATE OF DEPARTURE 1640
DEGREE MA
UNIVERSITY St John's College, Cambridge
LIFE IN BRIEF Greaves graduated BA at Cambridge in 1613 and he was the first-ever Master known to have been appointed to the newly chartered School.
He came to Almondbury in his early 20s and married Maria Crosland, the daughter of the vicar of Almondbury, in 1627. The School probably had no more than 20 boys in these early days.
It's believed that Greaves supplemented his income by also holding livings at Holmfirth and Tankersley, near Barnsley. He moved to Tankersley in 1640 and died there in 1677.

HEADMASTER FACTFILE 1608-2008

2

NAME Rev George Farrand
DATE OF APPOINTMENT 1640
DATE OF DEPARTURE 1680
DEGREE Unknown
UNIVERSITY University College, Oxford
LIFE IN BRIEF George Farrand was probably a curate of Almondbury Church. He countersigned the appointment of Sir John Kaye of Denby Dale as a Governor of the School in 1641, soon after his arrival.
He maintained the parish registers and was much given to including comments in Latin, prose and verse on important issues of the day. It was the time of the English civil wars, and Farrand, an ardent Royalist, reports in 1860:
'Charles the 2nd our most pious King (almost 13 years after the beheading of his father which by those Cromwellian monsters was perpetrated on 30th day of January 1648) is being restored, given back and returns on the 29th day of this month.'

occasions when the School was closed. In those days, schools were rowdy places, and a tranquil vicarage was preferable to a boisterous schoolroom. As Oliver Goldsmith once wrote, 'If you are for a gentle easy profession bind yourself seven years as an apprentice to turn a cutler's wheel, but avoid a school by any means.'

The School and the boys

King James's was a small school, as were many others throughout England in the sixteenth and seventeenth centuries. In small towns – and indeed villages – grammar schools existed, teaching Latin and often Greek. A grammar school building still stands in Flockton. In Ossett, Tadcaster, Ilkley, Otley, Scarborough and right across Yorkshire, there were grammar schools. For a decade there were annually only a dozen boys at Almondbury, and it was not until 1740 that a small schoolroom was built.

The boys came from different parts of the parish, almost all of them sons of gentry or professional 'near-gentry'. 'Not a weaver's son amongst them' was a common complaint. A certain William Booth walked over from Honley (was there ever a time when a Booth was not an Almondburian?). No doubt it was a hazardous journey home on a winter's night. When Thomas Gledhill became Master in 1685 his two sons became pupils and one of them subsequently went on to Cambridge.

After Gledhill's death the School closed for two years; then came and went Joshua Sagar and Abraham Walker. In those days, when a school had but one master its continuity depended upon his competence and his health. King James's often suffered in this way and pupils had to find other schools, for example in Holme.

The Statutes

It is doubtful whether many Almondburians have read the Statutes of the School which were framed around 1700. Set down on parchment extending for a length of just over 3m [10½ft], they specified every aspect of the School's organisation, curriculum and methodology. They are currently kept at West Yorkshire Archive Service in Huddersfield and when they go on display are worth looking at if only for the beauty of their presentation.

The Master had his responsibilities clearly defined. His classical background had to be impeccable. Above all, his discipline should be faultless: it would appear that the boys' sobriety and reverence were frequently conspicuous by their absence. For example:

The Scholemaster shall not at any time suffer any gaming, Joyning, clubbing or sending for Ale, Wine or other strong liquors into the Schole …

and

… no swearing, cursing, lying, strife …

A hard life!

The Statutes reflect in meticulous detail the educational thinking of the day, although they are permeated by the expectations of earlier times. They must be viewed in the context of a society in which basic literacy was the privilege of the few.

HEADMASTER FACTFILE 1608-2008

NAME	Rev Obadiah Porrit
DATE OF APPOINTMENT	c1701
DATE OF DEPARTURE	1724
DEGREE	BA
UNIVERSITY	Lincoln College, Oxford
LIFE IN BRIEF	The son of Robert Porrit of Birstall, Obadiah Porrit graduated in 1691, after which was ordained priest at York and curate of Cumberworth. In his later years, he became curate of Honley.

7

He was the first Master to take up his appointment under the terms of the newly drawn up Statutes of 1700 and undertook to 'be faithful and diligent in his office, and observe all ye Statutes that he is required to keep or die without any charge or trouble to the Governors of said Schole.'

When he died in harness in 1724, he was described as 'headmaster and yeoman' suggesting that by that time he may have become a minor land owner.

HEADMASTER FACTFILE 1608-2008

NAME	Rev A Hall
DATE OF APPOINTMENT	c1726
DATE OF DEPARTURE	1727
DEGREE	Not known
UNIVERSITY	Not known
LIFE IN BRIEF	A mystery Master, about which very little is known.

8

The Almondbury Registers record that in 1727 'James Kemp and Deborah Wood were married by Mr Hall, Schoolmaster of Almondbury, virtue of a licence granted by Mr Burton, vicar of Halifax.' A further entry, in 1730, records another marriage by the same Mr Hall, curate of Church Kirk [a township near Accrington].

Rev Hall's appointment may well have been of a temporary nature, pending the arrival of his successor, Rev Samuel Brooke in September 1727.

Cambridge where he had a brilliant career, was ordained, and spent many years as Master of Beverley Grammar School. (I wonder how he reacted to over-zealous wood-carvers?)

Obadiah Porrit was Master at the time (a gift to the nicknaming fraternity) and he remained so for 25 years. Then the School was left in the custody of a Rev A Hall for a year until the arrival of Rev Samuel Brook.

Samuel Brook

In 1727 the Governors appointed the youngest-ever Master, namely Samuel Brook. He was 19 years of age and still a student at St John's College, Cambridge. Since the Statutes and the Charter stipulated that the Master should be a graduate, Samuel did not

The triumph of Thomas Tatham

Despite the Statutes and the prevailing rationales of 'spare the rod and spoil the child', 'speak when you are spoken to' and 'the child must depart from original sin', there was always a pupil ready to challenge the establishment. Such an Almondburian was Thomas Tatham who achieved immortality one day in 1706 when he crept into the empty schoolroom and carved his name with great skill on the top right-hand corner of the Master's desk. Unmistakeably and without fear, he carved 'Thomas Tatham 1706.'

The front of the old desk hangs now on a wall of the Schoolhouse and the carving celebrates a pupil who, over 300 years ago chanced his arm and then went on to

Carving his name with pride: Thomas Tatham risks the wrath of his Master and throws discretion to the wind

the Masters who informed posterity that teaching at King James's was scarcely a financially rewarding occupation. In a letter to the Archbishop of York, Brook reported,

I have a small grammar school at Almondbury at 18 £s per annum . . .'

and later,

'I have been at a large Expence building a School house . . . A benefaction of 5 £s a year to the school left by one Israel Wormall was obtained by decree of Chancery in the year 1753 but I never yet could obtain either the annual payments or the arrears due upon it.

Succeeding Masters voiced similar complaints about their impecunity. Edward Hasleham (1771-1778) and Thomas Sedgewick (1788-1804) were both critical of the Governors. To make ends meet, these Masters cultivated not only the minds of their pupils but

Porrit kept a few hens, Brook some livestock, and Sedgewick made hay for his horse and his neighbours

also the land surrounding the School. Porrit kept a few hens, Brook some livestock, and Sedgewick made hay for his horse and his neighbours. When Sedgewick left suddenly and without notice in 1804, the Governors claimed that the hay he had wained was rightfully theirs. The dispute was resolved through a neat com-

assume office until 1732. Thereafter he proved to be the longest-serving Master, being at Almondbury until his death in 1771.

When he assumed office there were 12 pupils, whom Brook taught in the Schoolhouse which was beginning to show signs of disrepair. Largely at his own expense, Brook refurbished the Schoolhouse and had a Schoolroom constructed at the back of the house, on the site now occupied by the ODH and the corridor which separates it from the Schoolhouse.

Brook's curriculum was essentially Latin, basic literacy and numeracy, and the catechism. His three sons were pupils and one of these, Samuel, went up to Cambridge in 1751. During these years, the School had a good reputation and some pupils came from distant parts of the parish.

Brook championed many causes in Almondbury and in Flockton where he was curate. In his prime he scaled the hills of Lepton on horseback to fulfil his parish duties. Sadly, however, the vicar of Almondbury reported to the Archbishop of York in 1764:

. . . the poor man is so disabled by the Gout and other infirmities that no children have been taught for several years. Within these weeks there has come an under master to teach . . .

For some 44 years, Samuel Brook was a humane and scholarly leader of his pupils. He also rebuilt the School and was an eloquent champion of the aspirations of the Almondbury villagers.

Who owned the hay?

Obadiah Porrit and Samuel Brook were two of

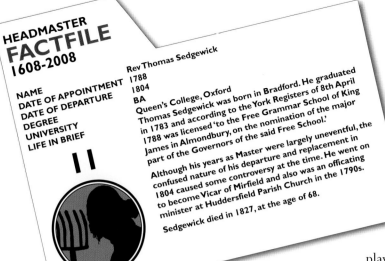

promise: the hay already wained was his but the aftermath was the Governors'! These were hard times for the defenders of our legacy not least because the Schoolhouse was constantly in disrepair and its maintenance was the Master's responsibility.

How did this affect the young aspirants to knowledge? The image of boys loading a hay wagon whilst gleefully quoting lines of Cicero or revising their declensions defies credibility – but it's irresistible to the imagination!

Another Smith arrives on the scene

One morning in 1804, Thomas Sedgewick left the School to take up a living in Mirfield, thoughtfully locking up the School and leaving the key with a neighbour in readiness for his successor. Apparently without any reference to the Governors (of whom only three existed at the time, all seemingly indifferent to their responsibilities), Sedgewick 'appointed' a friend of his called Foster. Foster – the 'Master who never was' – lived in the Schoolhouse for a few months and then himself departed, again obligingly leaving the key with a neighbour.

The Governors, promptly reminded of their duties, sought to remedy the situation by appointing Walter Smith as the new Master, the formalities being settled outside the Schoolhouse door because they couldn't find the key.

Walter Smith proved to to be an excellent appointment and he revived the School in many ways. He was 39 years of age, a graduate of Magdalene College, Cambridge, and had come to Almondbury as curate-in-charge in 1796 during the absence of the vicar. He enjoyed the patronage of Woodsome, which had at that

time passed to the Earls of Dartmouth following the marriage of Elizabeth Kaye to George Legge, the elder son of the first Earl of Dartmouth. For six years prior to coming to Almondbury Smith had been the Master at Slaithwaite School whose fortunes he revived in many ways. Not least, at odds with prevailing theology, he believed in the natural goodness of the child and there was therefore no corporal punishment for misdemeanors.

Interestingly, Smith had a simple covered playground erected at Almondbury where his pupils could 'walk, talk, play games not solely on inclement days.' This building – given the appropriately ecclesiastical name the 'Cloisters' – was later modified or dismantled to provide the School's pioneering 1868 chemistry laboratory of the same name (see page 87).

Smith lived at the vicarage, the first Master not to live at the School. It was a sensible decision, for the Schoolroom and the Schoolhouse were once again in need of repair. Between 1804 and 1821 Smith restored the School's reputation as a classical grammar school. He also had a small seminary at the vicarage where he prepared students for ordination. These young men also did some teaching at the School: one of them, James Goodwin,

became a permanent assistant for a while and there is a memorial to him in the Kaye Chapel in Almondbury Church.

Another ordinand was John Breay who came to Almondbury in 1816. In letters to his sisters about his work at the School, he said of his pupils:

They are an unruly set of boys for whom I have often prayed.

He also recalled,

One summer's day we went outside. We were reading Vergil when our attention was drawn by Armitage to a brightly coloured butterfly. The Trojan War was forgotten.

In another letter he wrote to his mother, telling her that on Sundays the School was opened to children from the village who were taught the catechism and began to learn to read.

The villagers are very grateful for our efforts, the children flock in great numbers, are very attentive and appear much delighted.

The significance of this provision becomes apparent when you realise that many of these children, aged seven upwards, spent the rest of the week working in the mills, in the mines or on the land.

The 'Armitage' mentioned by John Breay might well have been Richard Armitage of Deadmanstone, who attended the School between 1814 and 1821. In later life, he was to tell Canon Hulbert, the eminent theologian and former vicar of Almondbury Church, that he had often walked to School across the site of the 'chapel of old tyme.'

Smith died in 1821. His days at the School had been distinctive. It was better staffed than it had ever been, and whilst it still had only some 20 to 30 pupils it fulfilled its classical purpose and was integral to the village community.

Smith had whetted the appetite of the villagers for education. In November 1821, they presented a petition to the School Governors requesting that when they appointed a new Master they should:

… require him at all times to teach gratis such poor boys … as may be recommended by the parishioners in useful branches of education in addition to the Grammar.

Despite this being contrary to the Statutes, the Governors agreed. It heralded a change in the School's function and a decline in its academic reputation.

The 'English School'

The petitioners had triumphed. Almondbury Grammar School, as they called it, was no longer to cater exclusively for a minority who were to pursue studies that would lead them to Cambridge and, in most cases, to a church living.

The first Master under this new regime was John Coates. He was a non-graduate, curate of Lockwood, and son of the vicar of Huddersfield. He took up residence in the Schoolhouse in 1821. Since his

The strange mystery of the erroneous 1609

HAD YOU BEEN AN ALMONDBURIAN walking down St Helen's on a misty Thursday evening in November 1859, you would not have been surprised to see the lights ablaze in the schoolroom and the sounds of laughter, singing and applause from within. You would have known, as did the whole village, that the School was celebrating its 250th anniversary.

We know now – and strangely *they* should have known then – that the occasion was a year late. Why did Easther and his governors ignore the facts? If you look at Thomas Beaumont's letter, indicating his intention to bring the charter up from London to Almondbury, it is dated 28th November 1608 (he uses what is known as the 'falling 8' which was common at that time). Furthermore, a government commission investigating the state of English grammar schools in 1864, only a few years after the mistimed '250th anniversary', clearly gave the date of the foundation as 1608: a copy of the charter made by Samuel Brook had provided that date.

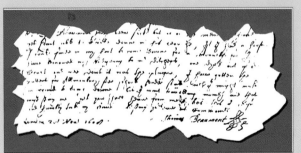

It has been suggested that the error stemmed from the fact that the Civil and Legal Year started on Lady Day, namely 25th March 1609. However, the date of accession of King James was 24th March 1603 and therefore the 'sixth year of his reign' fell within the chronology of 1608. The error persisted until the twentieth century: even the scholar Canon Hulbert and the historian Taylor Dyson did not question it.

What if on some auspicious day a daring scholar in Taylor Dyson's time had ventured to his study and, trembling, had said to his formidable headmaster, 'Sir, I think you have the date of our School's foundation wrong!'? And the Gaffer's reaction? That is best left to the imagination of those who were at the School in Taylor Dyson's time. At least, like Tatham, the boy's immortality would have been assured.

appointment did not concur with the provisions of the Charter, his father was deemed to be the official 'Master'. John was enthusiastic about his newly defined role and he admitted as many 'poor boys' who aspired to the basic skills as he could. Although there were, by 1826, still five boys who were pursuing a classical education, he had no fewer than 17 boys recommended by the parishioners.

These boys were highly privileged. Whilst the newly opened National (Church of England) School in the village admitted 100 boys and girls they each had to pay threepence a week, a princely sum for a poor family to find in those days. There were still many children as young as six who were already at work and whose sole education, if any, was in a Sunday School. Indeed, when we contemplate these fellow Almondburians it is salutary to recall the evidence given by one factory commissioner, surveying the working conditions of children (1833):

> *I have seen a little boy, only this winter, who works at a mill within two or three hundred yards of my door; he is not six years old, and I have seen him, when he had a few coppers in his pocket, go to a beer shop, call for a glass of ale, and drink as boldly as any grown man, cursing and swearing, and saying he should be a man as soon as some of them.*

Among those privileged Almondburians was a certain Godfrey Sykes, an eight-year-old from a large poor family. He had to surmount many hurdles to secure entry: he had to satisfy the parishioners as to his moral worth, and then appear before the Governors. Godfrey went on to become a prominent manufacturer and Mayor of Huddersfield. Speaking at a prizegiving, he recalled his gratitude for his years at the School and produced a copy of Pilgrim's

Progress which he had been given in 1827: a fair indication of his own progress in life.

John Coates saw his headship as a mission to improve the quality of life of the poor. In this respect he was successful, but the School's status was now in jeopardy. Church schools of various denominations and classical or commercial academies were flourishing and they had the resources to provide a better basic education than the studies offered by Coates. When he died in 1847, the boys dispersed and the School once again fell into disrepair. Silent, dilapidated, it stood on the verge of extinction.

KING JAMES'S RE-FOUNDED

Between 1848 and 1896 two headmasters, each remarkable in his own way, restored the character of the School which they 're-named' King James's School. They were Alfred Easther and Francis Marshall; and had they known each other they would surely have been kindred spirits.

Alfred Easther

One Spring day in 1846 the clouds were gathering over Farnley Tyas. Two men, one a man of the cloth and the other a man who owed his wealth to the cloth, emerged from a local hostelry having enjoyed a good meal within. They were approached by a farm labourer who, in passing, commented to the man of substance,

Sithe, maister Nowell, it's ossin t'slart. Best be 'oam.

The man of the cloth was mystified and sought clarification from his friend. The latter with a smile said 'It's for you to discover, but I think we should have brought an umbrella.'

The clergyman was one Alfred Easther, at that time curate of Farnley Church; his friend John Nowell, a mill-owner whose house 'The Wood' still stands across

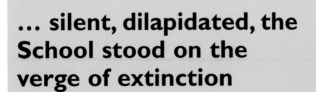

... silent, dilapidated, the School stood on the verge of extinction

the valley from King James's School (see panel). In Easther this incident and others sparked off a lifelong interest in local dialect and his *Glossary of the Dialect of Almondbury and Huddersfield* should be read by all Old Almondburians.

John Nowell: scholar, governor, businessman and philanthropist

JOHN NOWELL, born in 1794, was a pupil at the School during Rev Thomas Sedgewick's time as Master. Perhaps he even helped him with his haymaking!

He became deeply interested in science, especially chemistry, and at the age of 15 established himself as a 'magician' performing experiments all round Huddersfield. He wrote numerous articles which brought him in touch with leading scientists of the day like John Dalton, Michael Faraday and Humphrey Davy. Nowell was also a lover of the Arts, a classical scholar, a fluent French speaker, and a traveller around Europe and America.

Nowell's father, in partnership with other men, built and started Birks Woollen Mill, and John Nowell succeeded these manufacturing interests in 1841. He was a Governor of King James's from 1848 to 1869.

In later years, Nowell devoted himself to transcribing, in beautiful calligraphy, the Almondbury parish registers which had been neglected for centuries. Appropriately, this work was to be continued in more recent times by Harry Taylor, headmaster of the School from 1951-1973.

John's son, John Shearran Nowell, was also a pupil at the School before going on to Alfred Easther's old Cambridge college, Emmanuel. His early death, at the age of 38, was a blow from which his father apparently never recovered, hastening his death in 1869.

Nowell deserves his place in the Old Almondburians' Hall of Fame. As a Governor of the School, an inspirational member of the Easther-Jarmain-Nowell trio, a successful businessman, a devoted churchman, philanthropist and scholar, he left his mark to this day.

John Nowell lived in the family home The Wood which still stands today in a magnificent position on the southern slope of Farnley valley.

Within a couple of years, Easther had been appointed Master of the old School and a new era had begun. Easther was a Hampshire man who had proved himself as a distinguished teacher of classics and mathematics at the Huddersfield Collegiate School, in addition to his curacy at Farnley. His appointment was marked by the Governors making many amendments to the statutes. These significantly created a fee-paying scale designed to remedy the inadequacy of the endowments and to fund the School's imminent expansion. In the Spring of 1848 the work of creating a new schoolroom and dormitory began. The old schoolroom, built at the back of the house in Samuel Brook's time, was pulled down and a new one, with dormitory above, was built in 1848-9. The new schoolroom was slightly shorter than its predecessor in order to provide a corridor between schoolroom and schoolhouse.

Development of the curriculum

Easther taught Latin and mathematics and was assisted by a succession of ushers. He had, however, a strong interest in science, especially chemistry. It was an enthusiasm shared by his friend John Nowell, and by the headmaster of the church school in the village George Jarmain. All three went to the Great Exhibition of 1851.

In consequence, later that year, 'The Chemical Society of King James's Free School' was established with the objective of advancing the boys' understanding of this important branch of science. Easther had been teaching some chemistry since his appointment, but his facilities were very limited. Science at the time was very much the poor relation in schools, being deemed to lack the cultural rationale that a classical education possessed. For example, Eton did little chemistry at that time and only got round to building a laboratory in 1874 — some seven years after the one at

George Jarmain taught at King James's from 1852-1876

Almondbury. A former Winchester pupil described his science teaching in these terms:

The teacher began in this wise:

'You see these two pith balls?'

'No sir,' said some wag with his fingers to his eyes. 'I don't see any.'

Or as a variant somebody would say 'Two sir? I see three, sir' and so on.

There was an examination at the end ...
I obtained 8 marks out of 100, and was never a word the worse.

HEADMASTER
FACTFILE
1608-2008

14

NAME	Rev Alfred Easther
DATE OF APPOINTMENT	1848
DATE OF DEPARTURE	1876
DEGREE	MA
UNIVERSITY	Emmanuel College, Cambridge
LIFE IN BRIEF	Over 100 applications were received when the mastership vacancy was advertised following the death of Rev John Coates in 1847. The Governors appointed the 27 year old vice-principal of the Collegiate School in Huddersfield.

The original Schoolroom had been demolished just before Easther arrived, and his first task was to supervise the opening of the new Schoolroom (now the ODH) with its dormitory above. He also built the 'Cloisters' chemistry laboratory in 1868.

Easther died at the early age of 56, and 1,000 mourners thronged Westgate for his funeral in 1876. A tablet in his memory is mounted on a wall of the ODH.

This farce did not take place at Almondbury. By 1855 the boys were subjected to annual examinations set by Easther and Jarmain.

In 1853 the government established a Science and Art Department and awarded grants to schools whose pupils were successful in their official examinations. Jarmain himself entered for some of these and in 1858 he qualified in Organic and Inorganic Chemistry. In 1868 Easther had a laboratory built, largely at his own expense. It was a reconstruction of Walter Smith's covered playground, and it retained the name 'The Cloisters'. Designed by Jarmain, it had a tiered gallery; at the front was a demonstration bench and at the side were three benches where the boys could carry out their own simple experiments.

George Jarmain has been extensively chronicled and applauded. After his time at Almondbury he became Borough Analyst in Huddersfield, established himself as an authority on aniline dyes, and started a wool carbonising business with his brother in Kirkheaton in 1902. By that time he had a national reputation and was key witness to a commission investigating science education. A man of many talents, he was also an accomplished

musician who inspired music in the curriculum and in the School's various celebrations.

The tradition of excellence in science teaching and learning has continued to the present day and I am sure that Easther, Jarmain and Nowell would have beamed with pleasure when King James's School was designated a Specialist Science College in 2004.

Although still only a small school with some 25 scholars, the reputation of King James's began to grow. This was duly celebrated in 1854 when the Earl of Dartmouth presented a medal for an annual award to a boy 'of great promise and exceptional application to his studies.' Its first winner was George Edward Dodson. Where is this medal today, I wonder?

Evaluation

One summer's day in 1860 Easther was visited by a manufacturer along with his son whom he duly introduced. Speaking to his son, he said, 'This is t'chap 'at's to taiche thee, tha mun maund what he ses, and tha'll 'ave to go to church, sa tha mun behave thesen.'

What could this 'man of brass' expect for his money and what indeed would it cost?

- **Tuition:** 4 guineas [£4.20] per annum
- **Board:** 20 guineas [£21] per annum
- **Coals:** 3 shillings [15p] per annum
- **Library Fund:** 2 shillings [10p] per annum
- **Pens, ink, stationery:** 5 shillings [25p] per annum
- **Text books:** 13 shillings [65p] per annum

The total amounted to some £26 per annum. To purchase an equivalent boarding school education today, in a moderately sized school, would cost in the region of £10,000 a year.

So what reassurances could the School give to our aspirant 'man of brass'? An asssistant commissioner Joshua Fitch visited the School in 1865 as part of a national survey of grammar schools. His report concluded:

The Dartmouth Medal, awarded annually to a pupil of 'great promise' and showing 'exceptional application to his studies'

- The School was the only endowed school within reach of Huddersfield
- The School was growing in popularity
- Currently the School had 39 pupils, 19 of which were boarders
- Arithmetic, History, Geography and English Grammar were now in the curriculum
- Classics was taught well
- Chemistry was excellent. Science in the School was taught as an instrument of the highest value
- The boarders were well looked after by Louisa Ann Easther, the Master's sister.

All this must have been good news for the manufacturer and his son.

For the Governors, Fitch had this advice:

The school should aim at the highest academic standards. Not enough pupils are going to university. The school should not merely replicate what is best done in 'elementary schools.

... Some additions to the staff should be made.

The Governors responded. First, they appointed M Charles Feugly part time to teach French: the acquisition of modern languages in an area where the textile trade had foreign markets was more a matter of business than one of cultural refinement.

Secondly, in 1868 as a stimulus to the study of mathematics Thomas Jessop of Honley offered an annual prize of five pounds to 'the boy who passed the best examination in mathematics.' The prize has been maintained ever since, notably by the Old Almondburians' Society. This award, like that of the Dartmouth Medal, enhanced the School's reputation.

All Almondburians owe a supreme debt to Alfred Easther. Without him the School would not have survived. His scholarship, vision, and not least his business sense created a new school which, whilst not forsaking its responsibilities to the poor children of the village, attracted the middle, manufacturing and professional classes upon whom the School's economic survival depended.

Above all Easther created a new school environment. His wide interests – mathematics, chemistry, classics – led to the growth of the curriculum. His humane discipline, 'scorning the rod', teaching informally, mixing with his pupils, sharing their interests, created an ethos which within the schoolroom and the boarding community contributed to an enjoyable way of life. His is an influential memory. In every sense he was an authentic Almondburian.

It will be recalled that his early experience of the

Fenay Hall and the Brooke family

THERE IS NO QUESTION that without the financial and moral support of the Brooke family of Fenay Hall - and John Arthur Brooke in particular - the School would no longer exist today.

The links between Fenay Hall and the School go back over 300 years. Nicholas was one of the original six governors named in the 1608 charter; Thomas Fenay served as a governor from 1623 to 1626; and his grandson, also called Nicholas Fenay, served from 1650 to 1664.

Fenay Hall was purchased by John Arthur Brooke in the 1860s and he soon developed a close relationship with the School. The link had been established by his brother, Thomas Brooke of Fenay Lodge, who had become a governor in 1858 and would serve for no fewer than 38 years. A further brother, William, was a governor from 1881 to 1920.

John Arthur Brooke became a governor in 1877. Educated at Repton and Oriel College, Oxford, he was to become one of Huddersfield's most illustrious citizens: he became a borough magistrate in 1876, a county magistrate in 1877, and was made a Freeman of the Borough in 1919.

The School owes a great deal to the generosity of John Arthur Brooke and his brother William, never more so than at the time of the great financial crisis of the late 1890s when the School came close to extinction. By 1899, the School owed some £1,400 and the Brooke brothers agreed to pay interest charges for several years to allow Frederick Griffiths and his successor Robert Crump time to improve the situation.

It was fortunate for the School that, in the event, their faith was amply rewarded.

dialect of the district stimulated his research into the 'language and foibles' of those Yorkshire folk with whom he lived. One rent day when Easther, as was now his wont, was collecting dues from tenants of the School in the Woolpack Inn, he was mildly reproached by one man who thought that his rent charge was too high. Easther responded, 'Nay lad, a chap wi' a coit laak thine owt to pay moore. Tha's noan short of a paand or toathre.' It was memorable; it was typical. It endeared him to everyone. A thousand people wished him farewell. The School awaited such another to take up the mantle.

Interregnum

Why, one might ask, would a Welshman who was Vice-Principal at Caernarvon College choose to apply for a post at a small Yorkshire boarding school? Only Rev Thomas Newton could answer that question. One can only surmise that its antiquity and royal lineage inspired him. In fact, he stayed only a year, which was unfortunate in some ways since he seems to have been a strong, eloquent person who quickly established himself.

He inherited 26 boys from the Easther era; they were joined by his own son. What sort of place had he taken over? We do have an interesting review, reported by assistant commissioner D R Fearon who inspected the School in 1877. He described the buildings thus:

The house consists of kitchen, cellar, dining room, front and back drawing room (these rooms are low), four domestic bedrooms on the first floor and a good sized dormitory over the schoolroom. The dormitory is larger than the schoolroom and could hold about 12 boys. Using one of the above bedrooms, about 18 or 20 boarders might be accommodated. The schoolroom is fitted with gas and well supplied with old fashioned desks. There is a covered playground in the yard, but not at present well ventilated (known as 'The Cloisters'). There is a stable, two stalled, with appurtenances. There is a garden in front of the schoolhouse and a grass field with a steep slope, a part of it at the side of the school.

Predictably on the demise of a Master at the School strong representations were made by responsible citizens of the village to the effect that the School should open its doors more widely, especially to the children of the poor. In response, the governors recommended to the Charity Commissioner that 'a greater proportion of the Nettleton and Wormall Charities should be utilised for educational purposes' and that entry to the School should be open to boys from elementary schools in the parish. The Wormall Charity trustees decided that its income should be consolidated with the Almondbury Grammar School Foundation. These arrangements afforded entry to the School to more non-fee paying pupils.

Other developments in Newton's time involved the recruitment of more assistant staff even though there were only 27 pupils in the School. More significantly (in a non-academic sense) was the introduction of rugby football. Newton had a passion for the game and by the winter of 1877 there was a School Fifteen and a complete fixture list.

The future under Newton looked assured but – such was his eloquence and conviction – he was in much demand as a preacher. As a man of strong Anglican principles he abhorred what he regarded as 'irreligious, godless houses being erected by the School Boards.' Such a school was in the process of being established at the top of Fenay Lane.

And so it was that in January 1878 Shepley acquired an outspoken, strong-minded vicar. Meanwhile, the Grammar School awaited yet another leader who might fulfil its expectations, preferably with a rugby ball about his person …

HEADMASTER FACTFILE 1608-2008

NAME Rev Thomas Newton
DATE OF APPOINTMENT 1876
DATE OF DEPARTURE 1878
DEGREE BA
UNIVERSITY Trinity College, Dublin
LIFE IN BRIEF A Welshman, Thomas Newton was 33 when he came to Almondbury from his previous position as vice-principal of Caernarvon Training College. At the time, the School had 27 pupils, which included Newton's own son Arthur and two of his nephews.

Newton had a passion for rugby, which he believed helped in character building besides being an enjoyable recreation in its own right.

Newton soon became involved in plans to extend the School, although he did not stay long enough to see them put into practice. He blotted his copybook by launching fierce attacks from the pulpit about the 'irreligious, godless houses now being raised by the School Boards' and after 18 months in his post he departed to become vicar of Shepley.

15

Francis Marshall – the Reverend 'F'

In a speech to the Old Almondburians in 1900, the eminent old boy Craven Cudworth (see panel) recalled his first meeting with his new headmaster:

It was a lovely Spring morning. I arrived at the School early. Very few people were about. Then I saw a man seemingly gardening. He was a short stocky man. I took him for a gardener. As I approached, he turned and said, 'Who are you, boy?'

'I am Craven Cudworth, sir.'

'Ah,' he replied. 'Cudworth, the Cudworth, the boy who is the best mathematician in the whole of England!'

Cudworth's 'gardener' was none other than Rev Francis Marshall, the newly appointed head of King James's. Marshall was a graduate of St John's College, Cambridge where he had distinguished himself in mathematics. Prior to coming to Almondbury he had been vice-principal at Carmarthen Training College and headmaster of Wednesbury Collegiate School. It surprised Cudworth that Marshall should have been aware of the fact that in the College of Preceptors' Examination in 1877 he had come first boy in mathematics in the whole of England, a feat that he was to repeat in 1879, but it was an indication of Marshall's attention to detail and not least his affinity with budding mathematicians. As we shall see, he had an even greater affinity with rugby players.

An outstanding pupil in Newton's brief time, Craven jocularly observed later 'Marshall came with Euclid in his head and a rugby football under his arm.' Among the other locals whom Marshall inherited from Newton's time were Joe Wilson, son of the steward at Woodsome, John Broadbent, an innkeeper's son from Honley, and Harry Berry from the village. All three were subsequently to win the Dartmouth Medal, and in a letter from Marshall to the Earl of Dartmouth he reported that 'Cudworth (yet again) and Broadbent have come first in all England in the College of Preceptors' Examination of 1880' and that 'Berry has been second boy in all England in Chemistry.' This latter achievement was out of 500 candidates.

The School was rapidly building up a reputation. Many

HEADMASTER FACTFILE 1608-2008

NAME	Rev Francis Marshall
DATE OF APPOINTMENT	1878
DATE OF DEPARTURE	1896
DEGREE	MA
UNIVERSITY	St John's College, Cambridge
LIFE IN BRIEF	Francis Marshall came to Almondbury at the age of 33 He had the reputation of being an efficient organiser, a firm disciplinarian, a successful teacher and — like his precessor Thomas Newton — a fanatical supporter of rugby.

16

During Marshall's time, the School expanded and many new buildings were erected.

Sadly, things started to turn sour by the early 1890s. Marshall became increasingly involved outside School in controversy surrounding the professionalisation of rugby and there was probably more than a grain of truth in accusations that this was preoccupying him more than the School. As a rugby enthusiast he should perhaps have remembered the old adage about never taking one's eyes off the ball.

Craven Cudworth: academic and devoted Almondburian

BRIGHT, imaginative, athletic, hardworking, Craven Cudworth was the pedagogue's dream. He was 12 when the new headmaster arrived in 1878; at this time, he lived in a cottage near Birks Mill (later the family moved to the stone house which still stands at the top of Arkenley).

Having demonstrated his prowess in mathematics in the College of Preceptors' Examinations, he went on to King's College, Cambridge where he obtained a BA and MA.

Cudworth, who taught at Wellingon College and Leeds Grammar School, was a prime mover in the setting up in 1888 of the first society of old boys. He mainained close links with his old school and returned in 1923 to read the lesson on the sombre occasion of the unveiling in the Big of the memorial tablet erected in the memory of those old boys who had fallen in the Great War.

A devoted Almondburian throughout his life, he died in 1938.
The Rugby team with Marshall (in bowler hat) in 1884. Cudworth (inset) is seated second from the right on the front row.

of Marshall's former scholars came from the Midlands as boarders. By the summer of 1878 there were 34 boys in the School, 14 of them boarders. A year later there were 55, aged between 10 and 16. There was an urgent need therefore for more buildings. In 1879 the governors, with the support of the Earl of Dartmouth, decided to expand the School at their own expense.

Completed by 1880, the new buildings consisted of a classroom with dormitory and master's bedroom above; also added to the School were some kitchens with bed-rooms above for the domestic staff. The classroom has had various names over the years: it was once known as the 'New Lab' and later as the 'Junior Lab.' Today, it is a general classroom. The dormitory many will recall as 'Dorm 1'; today it is more prosaically known as 'Room 20'.

There was now a 30 yard [27m] gap between the schoolhouse and the new classroom and dormitory, thereby reducing the size of what had previously been a playing field. But this was not allowed to interfere with the boys' pursuit of sport: rugby, wherever, was regard-ed by Marshall as a vital element in the curriculum. To tackle, to endure a tackle, to scrimmage, to accelerate for the line regardless of those hurtling towards you – these were seen as supreme tests of character. The devel-opment of character, as well as intellect, had always been Marshall's objective. J N Tinker, a spry, cocky lad had this to say about 'Sir':

Before the match he placed the ball on the half way line and kicked the most beautiful goal you would like to see and he had long trousers on that day.

Others were interested spectators of the old School, not least the Charity Commissioners. D R Fearon, one of their assistants, visited the School and subsequently negotiated the administrative consequences of the new endowment arrangements made in Newton's time. These virtually amended the Letters Patent, the Statutes, and all the modifications which had been made since the 17th century. The principal change involved the establishment of six King's Scholarships and six Wormall Scholarships which entitled their holders to free educa-tion. Candidates had to be resident in the parish and to have attended an elementary school for the previous three years. Other provisions afforded access to scholars from the outer townships. Those villagers who had championed for a less exclusive School had cause for rejoicing.

Rev F Marshall to the rescue

'LAST CHRISTMAS I was invited by Greenhead College, our local sixth-form college, to read at their Carol Service. My passage was from Chapter 2 of St. Luke's Gospel - the announcement to the shepherds of the birth of Christ. The Principal of Greenhead College, a friend of mine, advised me to bring my own copy and asked that I read from the Authorised or Revised Standard Version.

'For convenience, I had intended to photocopy the relevant passage and slip it into my pocket in readiness for the evening. Unfortunately, that afternoon proved so hectic I completely forgot.

'My wife and I were just walking out of the house on the way to the service when my forgetfulness dawned on me. Now, my copy of the RSV is a fairly hefty volume. I did not fancy carrying this with me into church! It suddenly struck me, however, that I had a single-text copy of St Luke, the one I had used for O level Divinity in 1959 - 60. I raced upstairs and dragged it from behind the front row of books in my study, and off we went. In the church, I set it down on the rail in front of me, and the service got under way.

'Some time later, looking idly round, I happened to glance at its green cover and was suddenly struck by the name of its editor - Rev. F. Marshall. The identification was confirmed by the note on the title page: 'Rev. F. Marshall, M.A. – Late Exhibitioner of St John's College, Cambridge, Rector of Mileham, formerly Vice-Principal of the Training College, Carmarthen, and lately Headmaster of Almondbury Grammar School.

'It was a humbling and moving moment. Here was I, representing King James's as it were, about to read from a text prepared by my predecessor, whose edition I had owned in ignorance of its editor for some thirty-four years. It was an odd and rather disturbing feeling, one not diminished in any way by the reflection that hundreds and hundreds of boys and girls down the years must have learned their scripture from the Rev. Marshall's editions.'
Clive Watkins (Headmaster, 1985-1998), writing in 1994

Marshall was a prolific produc-er of text books both during the headship at Almondbury and in his retirement. Between 1870 and his death in 1902 he prepared 53 texts. Published by George Gill & Sons, they included a series known as the Oxford and Cambridge Manuals, an edition of the four gospels, editions of all the Shakespeare plays, and four mathematical text books. Additionally he edited several Latin texts, amongst them Caesar's De Bello Gallico and selections from Vergil and Ovid. In 1896 he offered a first and sec-ond year chemistry manual.

Progress

The years 1880-1890 were the great years of Marshall's time. By 1883 there were 76 boys on the roll, 30 of them boarders. In that year, the foundation stone of a major building project was laid by Blanche Brooke of Fenay. The new buildings would include a large schoolroom with open roof and a bell on the gable (namely the 'Big', later the Library) and a classroom (the 'Small') with dormitory and master's room above (later known as Dorms 2 and 3). Thus the School, as many will recall it, was taking shape.

The teaching staff was also being built up, with some notables like 'Penky Jim' Adamson and Max Grabner bringing stability. Penky was a jovial, brilliant second in command; Grabner taught French. One boy, J P Illingworth (who wrote some wonderful letters in 1962) recalled Grabner as a 'strongly built shortish man, all disciplined nerve and muscle. He did not wear his heart on his sleeve, but to any boy that cared he was was a kind and true friend.'

About this time Marshall married into a well known Almondbury family, the Taylors, who owned a woollen mill near the village. Another 'mother' in the line of many who had been in the School over the centuries, Mrs Marshall was, as one pupil put it, 'a gracious, kind and charming lady,'

What of those 30 boarders? What was life like for them? John Fisher was a boarder from Golcar from 1885 to 1887:

I slept in a dormitory over a classroom near the main entrance (Dorm 1). A dozen slept there. A strip of carpet was between each bed and a chair. At one end was a row of wash basins. In the middle of the room two large dressing chests. We were awakened by a maid about 7 o'clock with a bell. We had half an hour prep before breakfast ... We had prep 7-8.30 pm. At 9.30 slices of bread and cheese were brought into the schoolroom and [we] went to bed ... My home was at Golcar but [I] only went home at holiday times.

Sidney Barker, a boarder from Birmingham, remem-

Surprisingly, this small group posing in Fenay Quad in 1894 is the entire School of 43 boys at that time: the number of pupils on the register dropped alarmingly during the latter years of Rev Francis Marshall's time as Master. Standing, on the left, is Marshall's second in command, James Adamson ('Penky Jim') and the cloaked figure on the right is modern languages teacher Herr Grabner, soon to lose his job in a round of cuts as numbers continued to plummet

bered the cry, 'Bag the Bowls!' 'Usually,' he said, 'there were not enough washbowls to go round. Someone was late for morning prep!' He remembered wearing a round 'pork pie' cap with a gold and silver band round and a silver shield in front with the Almondbury coat of arms. Barker:

I am told you have trams running from Huddersfield. In my day you always had to walk ...

[It was 1889 before the first tram went from Huddersfield to Almondbury].

Barker described how boys went to the swimming baths in Huddersfield, running all the way there and back!

After the new buildings were erected new playing fields were acquired. Near and Far Arkenley had a rugby field, and in 1884 a cricket field was created. A long sloping field was tipped and levelled and the result was a small arena where the boys could wield the willow against the glorious backdrop of Farnley Woods.

Many will recall the grass tennis courts in front of the 'Big'. They were carefully constructed and maintained by the boys. J P Illingworth recalled:

We used to come out of school in relays and take our turn with shovel, pick and wheelbarrow ...

Running to town and back, rugby at Arkenley, cricket on warm summer days, tennis on their own courts, dumbells with a military man, Sergeant Handy – truly these were halcyon days. 'Mens sana in corpore sano'!

The two imposters

As we have already appreciated, those two imposters, Triumph and Disaster, have always lurked in the portals of King James's School. Had it not been for John Kaye's evasion of Edward VI's commissioner by moving the chantry chapel there might never have been a school. And what of Thomas Tatham? He seemingly triumphed unscathed. Yet Sedgewick had to go to law before he could keep his hay, and Samuel Brook – even though he had a Court of Chancery decision in his favour – never had the money due to him from the Wormall Charity. This pattern was also apparent in Marshall's time.

New buildings, new playing fields, triumphs in games with other schools, more staff, success in examinations, and more boys going on to university. Brownrigg went to Cambridge, Moorhouse to St Andrews, Carlton Oldfield went to Leeds where he later had a brilliant career as a surgeon. Beharrel, a poor boy from Almondbury Common, worked his way to the top in business and was in due course knighted for his services in the First World War. Above all there were many others who were to serve the village and Huddersfield in a range of professional and commercial careers.

From a flower decked platform in the 'Big' Marshall declared that the year 1884-5 had been the best in the School's history. Rightly so, for the number at the School had risen to 78, the highest hitherto, and the overdraft was negligible. High morale and confidence in the future were apparent when Brownrigg and Cudworth formed the Society of Old Almondburians. Brownrigg recalled their first reunion in the summer of 1888:

In the room (ODH) we met some whom we had not seen for years and with many a reference to days gone by we demolished the substantial tea set before us … and with song and speech and humorous jest whiled away as pleasant an evening as anyone could wish for.

However, decline, controversy and near disaster lay ahead. By 1893 the numbers had dwindled dramatically, the money owing to the bank was the largest ever, and the governors received a sharp report from the Charity Commissioners:

There are apparently about 36 scholars only attending the school. To teach them there appears to be a staff of one headmaster, three assistant masters and three occasional masters!

Why the sudden decline?

The Educational Act of 1870 had paved the way for universal education by legislating for School Boards (local authorities with power to levy a rate and build schools). A Board School was built at the top of Fenay Lane. It was well equipped and attracted many pupils who might otherwise have been admitted to King James's on scholarships. In Huddersfield, the School Board had started a Higher Grade School in 1894 with an emphasis on scientific and commercial education. The Technical School in the town opened its doors more widely. In contrast, only 12 new boys were admitted to King James's in 1895, and a mere 2 in 1896.

THE RUGBY RUMPUS.

THE REV. MASTER I——: Oh, fie, go away naughty boy, I can't play with boys who can't afford to take a holiday for football any time they like!
MASTER M—LL—R: Yes, that's just you to a T; you'd make it so that no lad, whose father wasn't a millionaire, could play at the game all in a really good team. For my part I see no reason why the men who make the money should'nt have a share in the spending of it.

*This cartoon in **The Yorkshireman** shows Marshall's high profile in the great rugby union controversy of the 1890s*

To some extent the decline was also the result of Marshall's excessive passion for rugby and in particular his opposition to the creeping professionalism which he felt was in danger of vitiating and corrupting his precious game. His preoccupation became an obsession, and soon he was addressing meetings nationwide, writing to the national and local press, haranguing people in pubs and employing every tactic to keep the game genuinely amateur. He abhorred backhanding and he was highly

... the charabanc conveying Marshall and the boys was pelted with sods, stones and other missiles

critical of the practice of giving talented players time off work to play.

There was strong resentment of his attitude amongst many people in and around Huddersfield. J P Illingworth recalled one day going through Elland on the way to play Rishton when the open charabanc conveying Marshall and the boys was pelted with sods, stones and other missiles by a furious mob.

In the end, his campaign failed. In 1895 the professional Rugby League was founded at the George Hotel in Huddersfield. His 'amateur' Rugby Union was to survive for nearly another 100 years, but it was little solace for Marshall. His disappointment was great, as was his sadness that many should attribute the School's decline to the time he spent elsewhere. In 1896 he left to take up a living at Mileham in Norfolk.

It was the end of a significant era for the School. As teacher, leader, scholar, sportsman and man of high principle and conviction, Marshall was an outstanding headmaster. Under him the School experienced great expansion and success. All those Marshallites who remembered him had no doubt about the debt they owed to his example and influence.

He was happy in the tranquillity of Mileham, where he continued to teach. After a few years, at the age of 61, he died. One final comment from a churchwarden at Mileham:

We still have one person, named Billy Cason, who can remember him and said he was always called 'Reverend

Marshall'. Billy was eight years old when the rector died. All the school children collected primroses and violets and made posies to drop in the grave as they filed past it. The grave is just inside the churchyard gate on the left of the path to the tower porch. The church was packed full for the funeral.

Full circle

On the departure of Francis Marshall in 1896 only 11 boys remained in the School, about the same number who were reputed to be in the care of the first Master, Nicholas Greaves, in 1611. A formidable task confronted any new Master on his appointment.

The new head was Leonard Frederick Griffith, 36 years of age, the first layman to hold office since the School's foundation. Shortly after his appointment, AF Leach of the Charity Commission described him as:

Decidedly above the ordinary run of grammar school masters. He is a mathematical man and, which is not unimportant in a town where non-conformity is very strong, a layman.

After his early education at Winchester Griffiths graduated from Magdalen College, Oxford. Before coming to Almondbury he had been headmaster of Mannamead School, Plymouth. As all the Marshallite staff except the redoubtable Sergeant Handy

HEADMASTER FACTFILE 1608-2008

NAME	Leonard Frederick Griffiths
DATE OF APPOINTMENT	1897
DATE OF DEPARTURE	1900
DEGREE	BA
UNIVERSITY	Magdalen College, Oxford
LIFE IN BRIEF	The number of pupils was down to 11 when Griffiths, a Surrey-born mathematician, took up his appointment, and only four of these were over 14 years of age.

17

It was a difficult time, and although Griffiths managed to boost numbers to 37 in his first 18 months the School started to lose out to other Huddersfield schools with better science laboratories.

Griffiths recognised the problem and even suggested that the School should become a 'School of Science'. But the Charity Commissioners criticised Griffiths' lack of business acumen and decided, after a mere three years, that the School required a new man at the helm.

had left, Griffiths brought with him Alfred Baker, an Oxford graduate and brilliant teacher of classics with wide experience. As events unfolded, Baker found himself increasingly in charge of the School. A later appointment was that of Frederick Powell to teach science.

Inevitably, within a few months of his appointment Griffiths was visited by a Charity School Commissioner

Leonard Griffiths, his wife and daughters with his entire School around 1899. At first, Griffiths did well: there were only 12 pupils when he arrived in 1897. But then numbers dropped away again and it began to look as though the School was doomed

(apparently all the commissioners enjoyed coming to Almondbury). In his report the commissioner summed up the state of 'this declining ancient school':

It enjoys beautiful and extensive views. The buildings are of a rambling and picturesque character. The furniture is somewhat old-fashioned. The laboratory is small and is of a very rough and makeshift kind. The times are hard financially, but funding is being reviewed. It would be a pity if the school were to be discontinued.

These sentiments were echoed by the President governor, John Arthur Brooke, at a prizegiving in 1898:

This school is a moral force, a distinct force, and we must not contemplate for a moment the failure of so ancient a foundation.

The expectations were great. Was Griffiths up to the challenge?

The first year was a honeymoon period. Numbers increased from 12 to 31. Amongst them were some talented pupils like Goldthorpe, Kendall, Woodhead and Maffin. They were all 'inherited' from Marshall. Harry Maffin went on to the Leeds School of Medicine and subsequently returned to the village where he was a much loved doctor for over 30 years. He was a devoted Old Almondburian.

Recruitment of pupils from the village improved, and there were some interesting newcomers from further afield. Perhaps the most celebrated of these was Griffiths' godson Felix Aylmer Jones, who was to achieve international fame as the actor Felix Aylmer (see page 91).

Of the 31 boys in the School only four were over 14 years of age. For many the School had become preparatory for education elsewhere. Felix Aylmer, for example, spent three years at Almondbury before going on to Magdalen College School and Exeter College, Oxford. He had some interesting contemporaries, not least Bob Sykes who arrived at the School from Lepton on horseback. Often he was accompanied by George and Fred Elliot; they put their horses in the stable 'at the corner of the yard opposite the kitchen and near to the back entrance.'

In the manner of Marshall, the School maintained its sporting tradition, although the winter game was association football. Felix Aylmer, who was no mean cricketer, had one interesting memory of a cricket match that never was:

We were playing Marston [did he mean Marsden or had he confused it with Kirkheaton?] The game was written off in advance as a certain defeat owing to the other side's possession of a bowler whom nobody could play. His name was Rhodes!*

Swimming involved a trip to the Ramsden Street baths, with fish and chips relished as the boys trudged back up Almondbury Bank.

It was a small school, but in Aylmer's view a happy one.

In his first year, Griffiths had clear reminders of the need to have adequate (and modern) provision for the teaching of science. The old ramshackle facilities could no longer match those of the higher Grade School. Increasingly the West Riding County Council was taking an interest in the School and was willing to help in the planning of new laboratories. Consequently, after much discussion with the Charity Commission, and the raising of appropriate funds (not least from the pockets of the Brooke brothers), the laboratories were built and opened in 1900. For many who were at the School before the Second World War, the new physics and chemistry labs provided good facilities for their scientific education.

Born in Kirkheaton, Wilfred Rhodes (1877-1973) was one of cricket's greatest all-rounders, scoring nearly 40,000 runs and taking 4,184 wickets over 37 seasons.

For anyone with a good pair of rose tinted spectacles the prospects looked good. Off stage however, as Felix Aylmer might have put it, all was not well. Leonard Griffiths had lost interest. The intensity of expectations

The end was nigh. The governors gave Griffiths six months' notice and at Christmas 1900 he left

and the urgency for immediate success depressed him and the running of the School was increasingly in the hands of Alfred Baker, his deputy. There were still only about 30 pupils in the School. Much campaigning, especially by the governors, failed to increase the numbers; the overdraft was growing relentlessly. Had it not been for the financial support of the Brookes the School would most certainly have been discontinued. Harry Maffin was later to sum up what he regarded as a rudderless school:

Griffiths was a man of limited ability, at least insufficient ability to revive a flagging school. He was himself quite a good teacher but had only half hearted interest. He was a sad man.

Across the road lived a certain Mrs Garner, whom many will recall. She stood in the wings of the Schol for many a long year and witnessed the unfolding of events both tragic and comic. She could have written a compelling history of the School; recalling Griffiths, she confessed: 'I couldn't understand a word he said!' His Welsh accent scarcely harmonised with her broad Yorkshire!

The end was nigh. At a governors' meeting in July 1900 they duly gave Griffiths six months' notice and, at Christmas 1900, he left. He had proved unequal to the exacting task of advancing the School at a time when survival depended on an increase in numbers. Nonetheless, his short tenure had seen the extension of scientific provision and the maintenance of a strong classical tradition.

On 5th December the governors met at the school and appointed Robert Simpson Crump, Assistant Master at Bath Grammar School, as their twentieth century man. Another challenge to another gladiator. Would the dust of the arena finally settle?

A new approach

Robert Crump, his wife, and his two children Marian and Robert, arrived at the School a few days after Christmas 1900. It was bitterly cold: the snow lay deep in St Helen's Gate. Their new home looked anything but picturesque. The schoolhouse had surrendered to cheerless neglect. Grates were broken, walls were peeling, and everywhere there were pools of water from burst pipes. Crump, a Yorkshireman, commented ironically, 'I knew I was back home.'

Robert Crump had his early education at Bradford Grammar School, whence he went to Queen's College, Oxford and graduated in Classics and Modern History. He had been teaching for 11 years, nine of them at Bath Grammar School. He had a deep interest in the Arts. He was a talented musician and at Bradford had shown a flair for drama. His son recalled many years later how at an early age he was acquainted with Bach and Beethoven, and that he and his father had read several of Shakespeare's plays together. Robert jnr became a pupil at the School in 1903.

Crump's interest in and sensitivity to the 'humanities' permeated his philosophy of education, and they were soon apparent in the staff he appointed.

Percy Coles was Crump's second in command. He had a first class honours degree in mathematics from Queen's College, Oxford. Like Crump

HEADMASTER
FACTFILE
1608-2008

NAME	Robert Simpson Crump
DATE OF APPOINTMENT	1901
DATE OF DEPARTURE	1912
DEGREE	MA
UNIVERSITY	Queen's College, Oxford
LIFE IN BRIEF	Former assistant master at Bath Grammar School, appointed Master at Almondbury at a salary of £300 pa with house. Son of Methodist minister and graduate in Classics and Modern History.

18

The School had 24 pupils when Crump arrived in 1900, but under Crump the numbers rose to over 100 by 1908 before starting to fall as a result of educational changes in Huddersfield. In 1912, Crump – beset by doubts about his ability to rise to the challenges ahead – decided to emigrate to British Colombia to take up fruit farming. It didn't work out, and he returned the following year to run a fruit farm in Kent. He returned to teaching on the outbreak of the 1914-18 war and died in Eastbourne in 1956.

he had a musical pedigree, reputedly as a violinist. Wooton, an MSc, was in charge of chemistry, and McEwen, a general subjects man, once played Long John Silver at the Theatre Royal on account of his wooden leg!

The School poses with Robert Crump and his family in front of the Schoolhouse around 1905. The teacher wearing a mortar board is believed to be senior assistant master Harry Lodge who taught mathematics and physics

In 1903 Bradley Shaw joined the staff and was to remain for 17 years. He was the archetypal art master: bearded, witty and wise; but above all he was well able to practise what he preached. F W Carter recalled how, on one occasion when the boys were out in the yard painting a tree, he was asked by Shaw:

'What colours are those leaves?'

'Green, Sir.'

Shaw mused.

'Carter, I see green, blue, grey, some red. Look more carefully. Don't just paint the obvious.'

This attention to detail was something dear to Shaw and indeed to Robert Crump, and it was in keeping with this aesthetic awareness that he and his staff sought to develop in the curriculum and ethos of the School. Much of Crump's vision was concerned with the humanising effect of the Arts. He had a clear understanding of what a liberal education entailed, but he was shrewd enough to realise that in a town like Huddersfield commercial and scientific studies and skills were essential. With the new labs and the new teachers he was confident that these subjects could be taught in a manner that departed from the merely formal acquisition of knowledge and involved the boys having an education that took them to the reality behind the words.

All these aspirations were evident in the first four years of Crump's headship and were given approval in a report produced by Michael Sadler, Professor of Education at Victoria University, Manchester. It was to prove highly controversial: Sadler had been invited by the Huddersfield Corporation to advise them on how best secondary education could be developed in the town.

In a long report he sought to indicate how he envisaged future policy. The following are some of his main observations and recommendations:

Technical education must rest upon the basis of liberal training ... In the training of every boy and girl in the community, the fundamental things are not the premature imparting of habits of manual skill and the 'breaking in' to a life of toil, but the quickening of the imagination, the opening of the mind ... First and foremost is the task of the schools to humanize ...

This was music to Crump's ears: it was the voice of a kindred spirit. Of the School, Sadler observed:

It stands upon a hillside overlooking a well wooded valley of great natural beauty. In its outward aspect it would appeal strongly to any sensitively minded boy ...

After a wide ranging survey of all aspects, Sadler recommended that Almondbury Grammar School should be developed into a first class secondary school for the boys of Huddersfield. Indeed, there could be no better

With the publication of the Sadler Report of 1905 the fur began to fly

investment and above all Huddersfield should aim at quality rather than quantity. At that time (1904) there were 50 boys in the School; Sadler envisaged over 100 with most of them staying until sixteen.

All this was massively reassuring to Crump. The future looked rosy, not least when his third child was born – only the second to have been born in the schoolhouse in its history. However, with the publication of the Sadler Report of 1905 the fur began to fly. There was strong opposition to the idea that the School should be

Arthur Eaglefield Hull

AN INDICATION of the School's good health during the early years of the Crump regime was the appointment in 1905 of Arthur Eaglefield Hull as music teacher.

Like so many other Crump recruits, Hull was a graduate of Queen's College, Oxford. At the age of 29 he had already established himself in Huddersfield musical circles and was later to acquire international fame as a writer on music, a composer and a much-in-demand organist.

Born in Market Harborough in 1876, Arthur Eaglefield Hull had a distinguished academic career and was appointed organist and choirmaster at Huddersfield Parish Church in 1904. He established the Huddersfield College of Music a few years later and founded the British Music Society in 1918. A prolific writer, his *Organ Playing: Its Technique and Expression* and *Modern Harmony* are still collectors' items today. Sadly, his life came to an abrupt end when, on 4th November 1928, he died as a result of injuries sustained when he fell under a train.

Although only a part-timer, Hull had a strong devotion to the School. In so many ways he enriched its ethos. Robert Crump jnr recalled that Hull – who knew all the Beethoven quartets before he was 10 – often used to organise musical evenings and was a colourful character with a great sense of fun. He had his place in the history of the School as well as in the history of music.

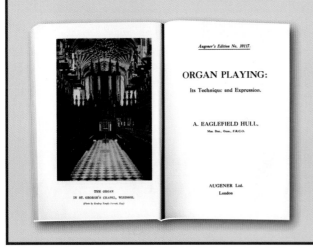

developed as Huddersfield's principal secondary school. There was much fury, much prejudice, and minimal dispassionate appraisal. Politicians, the National Union of Teachers [NUT], the Free Churches, industrial sceptics – they all raised their voices. It was a clamour Crump had feared but its intensity surprised him. If affected him deeply, and his health suffered. His daughter, Marian, recalled:

He sometimes came out of School looking ghastly and suffering very much. Somewhere in the background there was a bogey called the NUT which I used to think caused painful bouts of indigestion.

Sadler's proposal for the School was not implemented but the Huddersfield authority gave it increased financial support and its movement towards public control had begun. The School could now compete with other local institutions on equal terms. By 1908, the number of boys exceeded 100, with a few boarders. The foundations of a liberal education which Crump had laid were undisturbed.

The pupils in Crump's day

What of the boys? Were they influenced in the way that Crump and his colleagues hoped? Were they indeed 'humanised' in the manner envisaged by Sadler?

Sadler advocated 'quality', not 'quantity.' But how do you measure 'quality'? Much faith is involved. So many influences in art, music and literature are intangible. Any individual would find it difficult to articulate aesthetic and spiritual awareness.

A few tried. Bob Siddle, who was at the School in 1906, recalled excitement in his schooldays, especially in Eaglefield Hull's jazz sessions. He said that Crump was charitable about his feeble attempts at acting so that 'nothing was ever snuffed out.' Discipline, he said, was firm but fair. Crump was not a man for corporal punishment or harsh words, but he had a demeanour – a flash of the eye – which signified displeasure. One day, when Alexandra Mill was ablaze, the boys rushed out of school up St Helen's to watch. One master, a martinet by the name of Dr Lubke, wished them all to be punished. Crump demurred, saying that it was not every day that there was a fire!

Amid the hubbub Crump and his select band of colleagues kept faith and sought to make the School not just a place for high flyers but a community which recognised values beyond those readily discernible.

Much of what the School was trying to achieve was apparent in the Pageant of 1906 and the Old English Faire of 1907. Crump was principal organiser and script writer of them both. Held at Woodsome Hall and supported by Lady Frances Legge, sister of the Earl of Dartmouth, they involved the boys from the School and many of all ages from the village. Lady Frances had a great affection for the School and the boys were often made welcome at the Hall.

The summer of 1906 was given over to the pageant.

Crump, his colleagues and his boys put their talents on display in the drama, the music and the re-enactment of the Elizabethan period. Morris dancing, Tilting at the Ring were choreographed and rehearsed. 'What does Lady Frances think I am?' exclaimed Crump. 'A dancing master?'

Crump played the part of Sir Francis Drake, while Lady Frances herself took the rôle of Dorothy, wife of our first illustrious Almondburian John Kaye. But the show was stolen by young Harry Cragg who gave a virtuoso performance as court jester, an occasion made all the more poignant when a few years later he lost his life in the First World War.

A year later, Crump and his theatricals inspired another celebration. Lady Frances Legge's historical appetite had been whetted. Old Woodsome lived again.

The buntings fluttered, the marquees nestled amongst the trees, the musicians (several from the School) played on the terrace, well groomed horses waited before the landaus, and the gentry and ordinary folk mingled in a setting which had changed but little since the days of Arthur and his son John Kaye.

Both these creative and evocative occasions were but a preliminary to the celebrations to mark the 300th Anniversary of the granting of the School Charter by King James. Crump, like his predecessors, considered the appropriate date to be 1609. It was very much an 'Old Almondburians' event, organised by Lewis Cocking who had been a pupil in Easther's time and was to become a devoted supported of the School for the rest of his life.

On the morning of 24th November 1909 the boys, staff, governors and Old Boys processed in true Founders' Day style up St Helen's to Almondbury Church. At the organ was Tom Pearson, a

Robert Crump was the principal organiser and script-writer for the Elizabethan pageant of 1906 in which boys from King James's played a leading role and Crump dressed up as Sir Francis Drake. The jester, Harry Cragg, approaches in the background; sadly, he would later lose his life in the Great War

medallist from Marshall's time and now with an Oxford doctorate in music. Preaching the sermon was Henry Brownrigg who, in 1888, had formed the first society of Almondburians. He highlighted the School's Christian tradition and spoke warmly of his former Master, Francis Marshall, 'a thoroughly manly man, whose manliness appealed to the boys. He is remembered with respect and admiration.'

In the afternoon, the prizegiving in Huddersfield was an occasion not only for celebration and remembrance but also formal recognition of the new relationship between town and village. Crump delivered the keynote speech. He spoke glowingly of his predecessors, and with gratitude for the work of his colleagues. Pertinently and with a twinkle he commented:

The School might more fitly be called a Kaye cum Wormall cum Nettleton Grammar School than King James's Grammar School seeing that it owed that monarch only the right to enclose four rather barren acres.

A Festival Dinner was held in the evening. The 'Big' was filled with over 100 people, the oldest being Joseph Haigh, Mayor of Morley, who had been a pupil in 1860. Eating, drinking, singing, applause, laughter and endless reminiscing – what better way to celebrate the days of their (and our) youth?

Crump was well aware that this was his swan song. The years that followed were not happy ones. He had seen his vision become a reality, but he could not easily disregard the hue and cry roused by Sadler's report. He felt increasingly vulnerable. He sought a new challenge in which he could be his own man. A lover of nature, of mountains, of solitude, a Wordsworthian in his awareness of spiritual inspiration, he sought release from his academic responsibilities. His relations with his wife

Crump was aware that this was his swan song. The years that followed were not happy ones

were strained when he proposed going to be a farmer in British Columbia. In the end, he decided to go alone, leaving behind a daughter, Marian, at Cheltenham Girl's College, his son Robert jnr who was still at the School, a younger daughter, and a wife who enjoyed the security of independent means.

Crump said his farewell at Christmas, 1912. There was a genuine sadness at his departure. He had fashioned a school that had high academic standards. He had followed his star, and he had taken his colleagues and boys along a path of aesthetic awareness which, together with his strong Christian belief, formed the foundation of personal and social development. Perhaps historians have underrated him.

Within a year he was back in England. He and his wife took over a fruit farm in Kent. At the outbreak of the First World War he returned to teaching. In a letter, one of his pupils recalled:

Daddy Crump's leaving was like a bereavement – we could not imagine the School without him. An unassuming man. A fine headmaster.

GAFFER'S BRAVE NEW WORLD

John Thewlis and many of his schoolfriends were sad when Robert Crump departed:

We could not imagine the School without him.

Within a few months their imagination turned in the direction of a new headmaster. Thewlis recalled this new image vividly:

When Taylor Dyson arrived our first reaction was one of astonishment that he was so young ... He soon made his presence felt in various ways, but chiefly by his enthusiasm and approachability which were new to us. The outgoing and incoming heads were complete opposites – the one calm, extremely dignified, with silvering hair and aristocratic well-chiselled features – the other very young, energetic with bubbling enthusiasm and somewhat gingery hair and glasses. In a way it was symbolic ...

Taylor Dyson was 30 when he came to Almondbury. He was a native of Saddleworth and studied at the Technical College in Huddersfield for three years. In 1901 he graduated at Victoria University, Manchester in History (Honours) when he was 19, and he completed his MA in 1908. In the meantime he had also studied part-time for a degree in Modern Languages at the University of London. His credentials were impressive since he also held the Advanced Diploma of the University of Caen and an Indian Civil Service qualification. One might conclude that he had been a very busy young man!

Before coming to Almondbury he had taught for four years at Nottingham Boys' High School, then – as now – one of the finest independent day schools in the country. He was therefore well fitted as a scholar and as a teacher for the tasks that lay ahead.

He was married to 'Poppy', whom many will recall; and Beryl, his daughter, was just one year old. He fell in love with the School instantly and it was an affection which was to survive much hardship and disappointment in the 32 years that followed.

Most of the Masters over the centuries had had strong first impressions both of the Spartan and the Elysian. Taylor Dyson had this to say:

It was a fascinating, rambling, old-fashioned place with no pretence at either creature comforts or modern facilities. There was no central heating, but huge open fireplaces in the classrooms, very comfortable for the masters standing close by but none too comfortable for the boys on the back row. There was no electric light, not even incandescent gas, but just ordinary three-pronged burners – it was indeed the dim religious light. There were no WCs, but just a row of tub closets where the boys could sit and muse, hold conversations and philosophize. Yet in spite of everything it was a grand school, and life was happy, contented and fruitful of good results ...

Taylor Dyson sensed that he was part of a memorable continuity, to which he could make his own contribu-

HEADMASTER
FACTFILE
1608-2008

NAME	Taylor Dyson
DATE OF APPOINTMENT	1913
DATE OF DEPARTURE	1945
DEGREE	MA
UNIVERSITY	Manchester
LIFE IN BRIEF	Possibly the most famous 'Gaffer' of them all.

19

When Taylor Dyson arrived at Almondbury in 1913, the number of boys on the register was just 56; there were five times as many when he retired 32 years later. It was an unparalleled period of successful growth, accompanied by major building extensions.

But Taylor Dyson also had his share of disappointments. Having always envisaged the School developing into an independent boarding school, he was saddened by its transfer to Huddersfield Corporation in 1922. He also suffered a crushing blow when, after guiding the School through two world wars, he was to lose his own son Marcus following a period of active service with the infantry in India and Burma.

tion. In particular, he visualised the School retaining its independence and becoming at least a reputable, if minor, 'public school.' Some of his 'Rules' reflected this image, notably:

Straw hats worn in summer must have a hat band in the school colours. Boys breaking this rule will be sent home.

And then – in August 1914 – the nation and the School were engulfed in war with Germany. There were some immediate repercussions. The staff which Crump had so carefully recruited and nurtured broke up. Some joined the forces; Lubke returned to Germany. New faces appeared and almost as quickly disappeared. The stability and the unity were undermined; but nevertheless when the School re-opened in September 1914 there were 45 new boys bringing the total to 108, the highest ever. During the war years, the numbers steadily increased and by 1918 there were 190 pupils. In 1916 the first woman teacher, Dorothy Sanders, joined the staff and stayed until the end of the war.

One wonders how she regarded a Polish nobleman by the name of Felix de Woytkowski whom Taylor Dyson recruited with a fanfare that must have sounded distinctly far-fetched. Apparently, Felix had studied at the universities of Petrograd, Lvov, Paris and Oxford without graduating at any of them. In addition to being fluent in French, German and Russian he also claimed to be a graduate in Science and Law. Furthermore, he was an international rifle shot and an international tennis player.

Clearly Felix stretched credibility; but an eminent Old Almondburian Clifford Stephenson who was at the School at the time confirmed that de Woytkowski was indeed a 'legendary rifle shot at Woodsome' and that 'his tennis playing was a dream.' But he added:

He left in 1918 leaving behind him a trail of debts and many a broken heart amongst the ladies of the town.

Although many of Crump's stalwarts had departed there remained a trio of part-timers, namely Bradley Shaw, Eaglefield Hull and Herbert Graham; the last-

Taylor Dyson in his study, with his beloved wife Poppy. The School was to see remarkable growth during his 32 years as headmaster

named was a qualified Physical Education teacher who provided a more professional approach than Sergeant Handy's physical jerks. One of Taylor Dyson's principal recruits in 1917 was A E M Carleton, a teacher of Literature whose Irish charm and courtesy were to illuminate the School for 13 years.

If Crump's central ideal was 'aesthetic', then Taylor Dyson's was 'corporate.' He considered the social life of the School and all that implied as a fundamental feature of education. Learning from each other, sharing significant experiences both within and without the curriculum, cultivation of courtesy and respect, being willing to use one's talents for the good of others – these were all objectives which he and his staff sought to achieve.

He soon introduced the House System on the model

Digging for victory: squads worked in rotation, digging, furrowing, hoeing and garnering. The boarders found the 'bunk' fruitful territory for nocturnal raids

of the public schools in the hope that its loyalties could strengthen a sense of communal identity. All readers will respond to the illustrious House names – Dartmouth, Fenay, Jessop and Siddon. The latter honoured Emily Siddon who had become the first lady governor of the School in 1887 and was to continue to serve it in so many ways. Her affection for the place was never dimmed.

Taylor Dyson recalled that on his second night in Almondbury he was visited by three Old Boys – Harry Aston, George Garton and Harry Sykes – who wished to revive the Old Boys' Society which had become defunct in Griffiths' days. They were duly welcomed and supported.

The Great War was not, as many newspapers prophesised, 'over by Christmas.' Wars rarely are. Invariably, they highlight and strengthen social unity, and not least in the ethos of schools. Very soon the 'bunk' was converted into a vegetable garden and the boys at Almondbury were busily 'digging for victory.'

In 1915 a School Cadet Corps was formed. Joseph Wilson, who had been a boy at the School in Easther's time and then became the Earl of Dartmouth's agent, put the Woodsome rifle range at the School's disposal. Drill and route marches, tactical talks and simulated forays into no-man's land seemed like good fun, but their sombre significance was never far away, the warm comradeship being chilled by the implications of it all. These implications were stark. 'Men' who had been 'boys' at school only a few years earlier fell in futile conflict. The cout jester in Crump's pageant was killed in 1915, soon to be followed by Geoffrey Lunn, Walter Davies and Frank Quarmby. By the end of the war, 41 boys had lost their lives. A bronze tablet was erected in the 'Big' in 1923 commemorating them.

The main work of the School continued despite the inevitable tensions of the War. Very few members of staff stayed more than a couple of years before they too exchanged the tranquillity of the Farnley Valley for the turmoil of the Flanders fields. Taylor Dyson remained as a young father figure to all, and Carleton brought Shelley and Keats into the lives of many. He was by all accounts a remarkable teacher.

Taylor Dyson had his own style and it remains in the memories of those whom he taught. He was adept at the Socratic method – leading the class through a series of questions and answers to conclusions which they then worked out for themselves. 'What might have happened if Napoleon had won at Waterloo?' he might ask, and the process would begin.

His pupils were also aware of his tendency to depart from the theme and embark on some digression which invariably kept his listeners spellbound. His lessons were never dull, and his directions for specific reading ensured thorough follow-up. Clifford Stephenson recalled Taylor Dyson's comment:

It is more important to know the questions than to know all the answers. There are some who know all the answers but very little else.

The war years produced many a lad who was to fashion a career in medicine, law or the teaching profession; many others made contributions to the industry and commerce of Huddersfield that are still remembered. The School's links with Cambridge remained as strong

'Men' who had been 'boys' at school only a few years earlier fell in futile conflict

as ever: Archer, Jessop and the Appleyard brothers all followed the well-worn track.

One day, a chubby youth entered the Small classroom proclaiming, 'The War is over!' How did he know that? Whatever his source, he was right. The Armistice had been signed that very morning, 11th November 1918. The School rejoiced; but Taylor Dyson warned against triumphalism. Nevertheless the Marseillaise and the National Anthem were sung and various heroes were loudly cheered. The boarders, now numbering 30 out of a total of 190 boys, celebrated for many days. Amongst them was Gerald Dobson, a supreme Almondburian whose place in the School's Role of Honour is assured. We shall hear more of him later in this story.

The life of the boarders over the centuries warrants a book of its own. Here we must content ourselves with a series of recollections:

Gerald Dobson:

On some mornings there might be a snap dorm inspection. Just as you were half way through your porridge and thinking how good it was, your name would be called out. You reported to your bed space. Matron turned back the smooth, neat coverlet and revealed the untidy mess underneath.

Clifford Stephenson:

When the boarders weren't hungry they were ravenous. I've seen a boarder put away a two pound fruit loaf topped with sweetened condensed milk at one sitting – miraculously he still lives!

Joe Thornton:

I ate a lot of Gaffer's turnips in my time … !

In the aftermath of war there was a steady increase in the number of boys at the School – over 200 by 1919. New faces arrived, many of which would be recognised by the Taylor Dysonites still around today. A famous trio was appointed at the same time: Black, Burn and Blackburn. Black only stayed for a year, but Burn – a Welshman with a ready wit and a distinctive flair for

teaching mathematics – was at the School for the next 24 years. Blackburn stayed for 33 years: a meticulous, scholarly teacher of classics who was later to script and organise the famous 1936 School Pageant.

Eaglefield Hull left and was replaced by one of his pupils, Haydn Sandwell, who sustained the musical tradition established in Easther's time. Sandwell was to enliven the School for the next 11 years.

Between 1920 and 1921, three men were appointed, each highly talented and each to be responsible in the years ahead for the School's academic and social wellbeing. Leonard Ash had a first class honours degree in Modern Languages. For the next 30 years he was to bring his scholarship and humanity to generations of boys. He will be remembered by many.

John Hopton, a Leeds graduate, was a widely experienced teacher of mathematics and science; John Baldwin had degrees in both Arts and Science (how often did that happen in those days?) and had taught at Taunton School in Southampton for 17 years. He was to succeed Taylor Dyson as headmaster in 1945.

Arthur ('Joe') Hebron, a flamboyant and innovative teacher of science, served the School for seven years. One day he confronted a bright, perky lad from Shelley with the question, *'How do we know that diamonds and coal are formed from the same element?'* Quick-witted Shelleyite: *'Please, Sir, some who knaws poots it in books!'*

This same versatile Joe Hebron, whilst playing the part of Malvolio with Huddersfield Dramatic Society, 'sent even strong men hysterical!'

The growth of the School (200 pupils by 1920) meant that accommodation for all had become impossible. Between 1919 and 1923 use was made of the Wesleyan schoolroom in the village. For four years, boys and masters trudged up and down St Helen's and used whatever rooms and trestle tables were available. It was a fight against fatigue and a challenge to maintain standards of work. The challenge was particularly great, for schools generally were having to adapt to the

Taylor Dyson's staff in 1920, by which time the School had 200 boys.
Back row: A Hebron; L Bower; H Blackburn; J M Tyas
Middle row: R Burn; Miss J E St Clair; Taylor Dyson; Miss M A Waterhouse; A E M Carleton
Front row: L C Ash; J I Hopton

new system of School Certificate and Higher School Certificate: these examinations had been introduced in 1917.

The main school course led up to School Certificate and Matriculation (the latter being a requisite for entry to university). For those boys who stayed on after 16, there was a Sixth Form working for a Higher School Certificate.

Generally, schools had a Science Sixth (usually Mathematics, Physics and Chemistry) and an Arts Sixth (Classics, Modern Languages, English and History). At Almondbury the sole Sixth Form course until 1930 was Science. The old classical tradition had faded; the mathematics/science one, evolved through the years of Easther, Jarmain and Marshall, remained strong.

I was the sole member of the first year Arts Sixth in 1938. The statistics below show clearly the very limited growth of the Sixth Form at King James's before the Second World War in relation to the growth of the School as a whole:

Date	Total	Total Sixth Form	Science	Arts
1913	56	4	4	0
1916	140	2	2	0
1917	172	2	2	0
1921	237	8	8	0
1925	255	8	8	0
1927	261	7	7	0
1930	216	10	8	2
1936	260	13	9	4
1940	310	16	12	4
1945	315	22	18	4
1951	325	30	20	10

These figures are particularly disappointing when the development of secondary education locally is considered. The College in New North Road had over 400 pupils in 1905. In 1909 Greenhead High School was opened and soon had 400 girls. In 1921 Royds Hall School was opened. The omens were clear: the future lay not in the development of a small independent school but one which was locally controlled and locally funded.

Taylor Dyson mused upon these inevitabilities as he walked over to his beloved Woodsome or watched the School cricketers at Arkenley:

I have had my dreams and my visions, but mostly in the solitude of the wilderness ...

His ideal was worthy, but it did not measure up to reality. In the summer of 1922 the decision was made to hand the School over to the Huddersfield Corporation. No more rent days at the Woolpack! Tenants now went to the town estate office!

As Easther might have said to one of the tenants, in a dialect he had humorously acquired, 'Ee, lad, tha's missin' summat!'

Dreams and Realities

By 1923 the boarders had gone, except for a few who lived with the Dysons in the schoolhouse. The dormitories had been converted into classrooms. The middle dormitory became two classrooms (Dorms 2 and 3). An iron staircase was built on the outside wall of Dorm 3 to admit boys to the classrooms upstairs. The Small was enlarged. Electric lighting was installed. The schoolhouse, which had been the bane of many a Master over the centuries, was greatly improved. In 1924 a covered playground to the rear of the schoolhouse was converted into a dining room. The old stables and outbuildings were reconstructed as kitchen, pantry and servery. There was now accommodation for over 100 diners and 'sandwich baggers.'

The changes went on steadily: new staff were appointed and by 1924 there were 10 full-time staff (and the headmaster), three part-timers and 250 boys. They were years of transformation, the likes of which had never been seen before.

Caretakers have their place in the history of schools, not least in the history of King James's. They all have their foibles; they all have a dusty, sweeping, polishing perception of what schools are about! 'Jim' was caretaker for 16 years from 1913 and could have come straight out of a Dickens novel. Gerald Dobson recalled:

In appearance he was somewhat grotesque having a huge hump under his right shoulder. On the left side of his neck was a fleshy growth the size of a man's fist. His standard garment over his shirt was an open waistcoat and his shirt sleeves were rolled up permanently. He had swept up so much that his whole appearance was dusty.

What a history he could have recorded!

From the dust of 'Jim' to the dust of the arena. How did Taylor Dyson react to the new regime? He took his disappointment well. He now had a larger school. It was a unified community. The house system flourished. Gilbert and Sullivan operas had become established as an

The first Gilbert and Sullivan opera was a performance of **HMS** Pinafore in 1921 and it became an annual tradition for the following 30 years. This was the cast of Mikado on a rainy day in 1924

annual event, as had school parties in the summer. In 1923 Sandwell took a party to Colwyn Bay and during the 1930s Taylor Dyson organised holidays in boarding schools in the south of England.

Academic standards continued to rise, despite the problem of early school leaving. At the prize giving of 1924, Taylor Dyson's optimism was reflected in his assertion that while the past had been 'glorious' the best was yet to come.

The School was still short of facilities. Physical Education, for example, was limited, consisting largely of a short weekly visit to the Arkenley playing field and a few 'physical jerks' in the Big with the desks pushed back to provide space. Boys who possessed white flannels and knew how to play graced the tennis courts, and the occasional swim at Ramsden Street Baths was a possibility for a few.

Things improved in 1924 when Walter Haigh joined the staff. He was a qualified Physical Education teacher with several years' experience; in 1936 he became full-time and ultimately spent the rest of his career at King James's. In later years he taught junior mathematics, became a Form Master and a passionate Fenay House

Master. Shrewd and forthright, he influenced more boys in his prime than he ever realised.

The School now had 250 pupils, the majority of whom left at 14. The Arts Sixth was non-existent. Clearly, the demand for scientific subjects was understandable: the tradition was there, and local attitudes favoured it. Nevertheless, there were talented teachers of French, English and History (Taylor Dyson, no less) and it was surprising that an Arts Sixth did not emerge sooner. In 1938, when I was the only member of the Arts Lower Sixth, the Upper Sixth consisted of Norman Kerrod and Geoffrey Lumb. Their quality reinforced the view that the Arts Sixth was in need of expansion.

As we have already noted, Taylor Dyson visualised his School as a community and a way of life, and he sought every opportunity to reinforce his vision. He rarely forgot a day for celebration or remembrance – Empire Day, Armistice Day, Shakespeare's birthday and many others.

He made much of the latter in his early days. The School choir sang a Shakespeare song. Masters and boys wore medallions of the bard. What a great idea!

However, what most will recall is Founders' Day. It was a suggestion made by Taylor Dyson to the Almondburians' Society in 1929. He envisaged a rally of boys, fathers and masters 'on the Sunday nearest 24th November' as a day of thanksgiving and renewal. Thus the first Founders' Day took place in 1929.

Many will recall Founders' Day. Many will

'Jim' (inset) leans on his broom in the school yard in 1937. The laboratories on the right would shortly be demolished as part of the School's expansion in 1938/9

remember long processions, winding up St Helen's, passing Kirk Royd, the site of the 'chapel of old tyme' which Arthur and John Kaye 'dyd shifte' in 1547, past the well, past Wormall Hall, and into the church.

In 1937 a full inspection of the School took place. The inspectors recorded many favourable impressions of the staff and the pupils. They recognised an ancient school in need of modernisation and expansion. They were particularly critical of early leaving and the absence of an Arts Sixth Form, and they stressed the need for better library facilities.

Within a few months of their visit the process of pulling down the old and building the new began.

The first phase involved the felling of the trees on the bank at the back of the School: it seemed like vandalism but it was deemed necessary.

Easther's 1868 laboratory, by now a humble cloakroom, was next. It's a pity that it was not spared: its historical associations warranted it. Down went the antiquated Art and Craft Room and the crude outside

Old Almondburians with memories of Walter Haigh as a cigarette-smoking Form Master, Fenay House master and junior mathematics teacher may be surprised to learn that he joined the School in 1929 as a part-time Physical Education teacher. Here, now a full-timer, he puts his pupils through their paces in the recently completed gymnasium/hall in 1940

latrines; and finally down went the 1900 science laboratories. The new buildings were completed by the summer of 1939 and consisted of two new laboratories (with three classrooms and new staff room above), an art room, a separate handicraft room, a large gymnasium/assembly hall and civilized washing and toilet facilities.

As a result of these developments, the 'Big' of 1883 – a source of so many memories, not least of the headmaster's oratory – became a Library, replacing a 'cupboard of books.' So it was to be, and so it remains today, with its own librarian and a range of associated resources. The room, as many will recall, is graced by a

'My one sentence "That's a fine idea, Squire" brought the house down'

Gerald Hinchliffe was a 'townsman of Almondbury' in the 1936 pageant. He recalls the occasion with pride

TAYLOR DYSON was a lover of historical enactment. So it was that in 1936 he had the idea of a pageant 'recreating' the history of the School. 'Tich' Blackburn wrote the script for a pageant in nine episodes, involving the whole School as well as children from the local elementary schools.

Blackburn produced a four-day masterpiece, combining music, prose, verse and dialect which, allied to the fanfares, music, costume, lighting, dancing and the sheer gregariousness of mass pageantry, was to attract over 1,000 people each day.

It was staged in a corner of the cricket field near Upper Arkenley Lane and much has been written about it: Norman Blezard as the ethereal, green-haired guide to the centuries; W B Quarmby as King James; Ian Hepworth as his Queen; and the superb casting of Willie Evans as a much-whacked schoolboy. Poor Willie was to suffer greatly during the war which was to follow.

Edward Akroyd devised the sets, Harry Gledhill the music and Blackburn wrote the new School Song 'Floreat Scola' which was to be 'rendered' ever afterwards at Almondburian dinners, speech days and other major School occasions.

Memories abound of a superb historical extravaganza. I played the part of a townsman of Almondbury, speaking just one sentence, 'That's a fine idea, Squire' which brought the house down.

Episode 3.   TRANSLATION OF THE SCHOOL TO
ITS PRESENT SITE.

CHARACTERS :—

John Kaye, Esquire, of
    Woodsome.........................S. Hallam.
Arthur Kaye, his son......................C. B. Wrathmell.
Clerk to John Kaye ....E. A. Barnes.
Townsmen of Almondbury ....R. Barker, T. Barker, D. A. Bowen, R. Brook,
            G. E. Cockroft, V. H. Ellis, N. Garside, R. P.
            Goddard, C. Hartley, H. Hartley, G. Hinchliffe,
            H. Holloway, N. Horsfield, J. R. Ireland, K. S.
            Jepson, N. Kerrod, R. A. Oxley, M. B. Peace,
            J. R. Poulter, D. Scouller.
SCENT: THE OLD CHAPEL YARD IN ST. HELEN'S LANE, ALMONDBURY.
TIME: 1547.

stained glass window incorporating the School Crest designed and executed by Edward Akroyd in 1940.

All these changes took place midst the rumblings of imminent war. So it was, as the new buildings were occupied, that once again the country was at war with Germany. In a beautiful book, again the work of Edward Akroyd, the names of the 35 Old Boys who died in the war are inscribed on vellum; and an oak bookcase designed by Robert Thompson of Kilburn stands as a memorial. Many of my own friends, my contemporaries through School, gave up their lives. They are still remembered and honoured, and they are poignant reminders of the realities of war.

By 1944 the end of the war seemed in sight and thoughts were turned to post-war reconstruction in every area of national life. Reform in education was long overdue and in 1944 an Education Act was passed whereby all pupils from the age of 11 were to have a secondary education according to ability and aptitude.

Accordingly, each local authority was to produce a Development Plan. Most envisaged a tripartite system of grammar schools, technical schools and secondary modern. They were based on the principle – nowadays disputed – that at the age of 11 it was possible to identify distinct academic, technical or 'general' aptitudes; but nonetheless the system provided a framework for progress.

Taylor Dyson had many anxieties about what lay ahead for his School. Was its destiny again at risk? He also had to contemplate his own future. He had now completed 32 years' service. Soon, he knew, he would have to bid farewell to his School. Consequently he decided that in the summer of 1945 he would retire.

Taylor Dyson ranks amongst the greatest of the headmasters of the School. At a dinner long after his retirement, one Old Almondburian asserted that Easther, Marshall and Taylor Dyson were those who had had the greatest influence on the survival and evolution of the School. Many readers will recall the Gaffer as a leader, one who could induce pride, shame, determination or *esprit de corps* with a turn of phrase or simply by his stance. No one doubted his honesty and sincerity. Always he was concerned for the welfare of his boys.

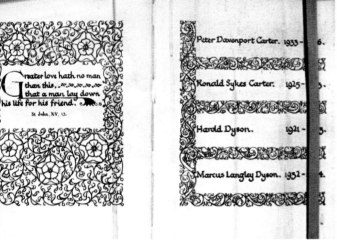

(Top): Edward Akroyd's magnificent stained glass window in the Library. Note that it carries the 'wrong' date of 1609 for the School's charter in keeping with the misconception at that time
(Bottom): Akroyd's book in vellum, still on display in the library, open at the page recording the death of Marcus Dyson

Their personal and social development mattered to him just as much as their academic development. 'Aim high,' he would say, 'and aspire to things beyond your reach.'

I was the only one studying History with Taylor Dyson in the Sixth Form in 1938. Always he challenged me and insisted on substantial reading and research. He treated me like a potential undergraduate. It is, therefore, a mystery that, as such a good teacher at that level, he did not initiate history in the Arts Sixth much earlier.

There are many who have taken Almondbury and its School into their hearts and minds. This was certainly true of Taylor Dyson. The village, the church, country houses and historic links – these were all food for his soul. In his speeches, writings and demeanour he was an archetypal Almondburian. He gave his time, energy and talents to many causes, but his thoughts and hopes returned unfailingly to that 'scole howsse' at the foot of St Helen's Gate. He was its champion, its guardian, its articulate advocate. A fine man. An outstanding headmaster.

And so it was in the summer of 1945 he bade farewell to it all. The School assembled for the last time in his presence. The old school bell which had been silent since 1939 tolled once again in his honour. John Baldwin spoke of his long service, his supreme example and the sadness of parting. The 'Gaffer' replied and, as always,

commanded rapt attention. This was his last class. In his 32 years he had seen many changes and had often had to bow to the inevitable, seeing the precious fabric of his dreams in shreds. But he had always sought to keep alive the honourable tradition of the School. He asked everyone to remember the School in good times and in bad, to find inspiration in the past, pride in the present, and hope and faith in the future.

'Floreat Schola' was sung; Auld Lang Syne followed, and Taylor Dyson left the hall for the last time.

Taylor Dyson and his wife Poppy retired to Christchurch. He spent a rich retirement in its community, teaching, speaking and writing, and he died in the spring of 1957 at the age of 73.

The Struggle for Status

By the time John McLean Baldwin took up the mantle of headmaster of Almondbury Grammar School (its traditional name at that time) there was trouble brewing in the council chamber in Ramsden Street. Baldwin had taught Physics at the School for 24 years. He was a man of many talents and broad sympathies: both Shelley and Archimedes were his 'friends.' A lover of music, a craftsman, a youth leader and a man of dignity that commanded respect, he was an ideal successor to Taylor Dyson. His

Fred Hudson - geographer, teacher and second master *par excellence*

FRED HUDSON, a Yorkshire-born first class honours graduate of Leeds University, was a towering figure for 37 years. He joined the School in 1935 and it proved an excellent appointment: not only did 'Soapy' Hudson bring scholarship and lecturing flair to the School but he also established himself over the years as the quintessential Almondburian.

Under Hudson ('Soapy'), geography became more practical, more realistic and more educationally valuable. Physical geography was one of his particular strengths; he was a superb cartographer, and his blackboard maps were works of art. His lessons were often spellbinding.

Fred Hudson was also a keen student of history and archaeology, and it was entirely fitting that he should have been the leader of the group of boys – all members of his own Surveying Society – who were destined to 'rediscover' the School Charter in 1952. He was also a talented pianist and music lover.

Hudson served under four headmasters and was to become Second Master on the retirement of Leonard Ash in 1953. He was a stalwart supporter of the Old Almondburians' Society (did he ever miss a Dinner or other Old Almondburians' event?). Like so many of his predecessors he found the School, its history and its charm an inspiration.

Fred Hudson (front right) with headmaster Harry Taylor at a prefects' meeting in 1954. Left to right: C Goldsmith; G Gelder; R Byrom; I Shaw; T Stocks; A E Sykes; N Schofield; J M Sykes; F Shaw

accession signified the end of the headmaster living in the schoolhouse, and its rooms acquired new functions. Baldwin took over the living room as his study, its outside door opening directly on to the garden, and the family drawing room became his secretary's office. In a way, it was a return to the 17th century, when the house was the School.

Having been at the School for so many years it did not take Baldwin long to revive all those activities that had lain dormant during the war years. School activities, ranging from gardening to chess, flourished. Every boy had to belong to one. A new society, the Jacobean Society, named after the School's founder, was set up to stimulate interest in literary, scientific and debating interests; it was to play a colourful part in School life for many years.

HEADMASTER FACTFILE 1608-2008

NAME	John McLean Baldwin
DATE OF APPOINTMENT	1945
DATE OF DEPARTURE	1948
DEGREE	BSc; BA
UNIVERSITY	Manchester and London
LIFE IN BRIEF	

20

John Baldwin originally joined the School in 1921 to teach Physics . Having graduated in both arts and sciences, he was a man with a wide range of interests and talents. He taught English for two years and it was said that he 'could quote Shakespeare as readily as Mr Blackburn.' He was also a music lover and a craftsman with plane and saw; for some years he shared with Mr Akroyd and Mr Burn the role of Stage Carpenter for the annual Gilbert and Sullivan productions.

He knew the School intimately and proved the ideal figure to uphold the traditions and standards long established by his predecessor Taylor Dyson.

All the sporting activities also returned and produced such notable athletes as Derek Ibbotson and Jeff Taylor, whose successes are recorded elsewhere in this book.

In so many ways, Almondbury Grammar School led the post-war way, not least as the Old Almondburians' Society flourished once again. There was rejoicing in a new world – tinged with sorrow at the loss of those friends whose sacrifices had made it possible.

Meanwhile, what of the rumblings in Ramsden Street? In January 1946, the first instalment of the Huddersfield Development Plan was made public. It was not good news for the School:

Neither Greenhead nor Huddersfield College is capable of meeting the requirements of a grammar school with a four-form entry under the new building regulations. New sites are therefore needed. The present Almondbury Grammar School is

also too small, and the site is not capable of expansion, as far as the buildings are concerned, without undue expense. The suggestion of two separate-sex grammar schools would have additional advantages, if adjacent sites could be found for the two schools. Such a joint site would have to be 43 to 48 acres, and can be provided along New Hey Road. If two schools are accepted to cover the grammar school problems, the name "Almondbury" or alternatively "King James" might be transferred to the boys' school. Alternative uses can easily be found for the sites and buildings of existing secondary schools.

One of the alternative uses being mooted was that Almondbury Grammar School should become a secondary modern school. It brought a chill to every Almondburian's heart.

What were the valid objections to this plan? First, as has since been proved, expansion of the existing local grammar schools (both in terms of buildings and playing fields) was neither impossible nor uneconomic. Secondly, the existing grammar schools were communities of masters and pupils with traditions of their own and standards of work built up over varying periods of time. They were influential communities within the common culture of the area, and there were established attitudes towards them in the community outside. It is the basis of that confidence which nourishes educational evolution. As Michael Sadler had pointed out in 1904:

Every secondary school, however well equipped, must slowly win its way to public confidence. A successful system of education cannot be improvised or created by a mere stroke of the pen. It must grow. It must prove its value and slowly gain the trust of the public.

'The present Almondbury Grammar School is too small and the site is not capable of expansion'

It was lack of confidence which roused general opposition in Huddersfield to the authority's proposals. Almondbury had always possessed powerful local allegiances and the deprivation of a particular kind of school and its transplanting to the other side of the town were tantamount to removing the village church.

The opposition was spearheaded by the Old Almondburians' Society. 'Ike' Chambers, chairman of the Society and back from the war, protested strongly. A petition was drawn up and submitted to the Minister of Education. The local MP expressed sympathy with the case. HM Inspectors visited the School and could see no legitimate reason why the School could not be expanded on the present site. Taylor Dyson fired a salvo in the press.

However, the knight in shining armour in the battle was Gerald Dobson. Gerald Dobson had been a boarder both before and after the local authority's acquisition of the School. There have been few who have matched his devotion to its welfare. At a meeting at the Ministry of Education in June 1948, Gerald and Old Almondburian Ben Wortley, Professor of Jurisprudence at Manchester University, presented the case for the retention of the School as a grammar school. It was based on a well reasoned and substantiated document which Gerald had produced, and the Minister was both impressed and sympathetic. There for some time the matter rested, but it was now clear that in their further deliberations the local authority could scarcely disregard the strong case, supported in principle by the Ministry of Education, for the retention of the School's status.

John Baldwin's teaching staff of 1948 pose in front of the Schoolhouse.
(Back row): N L Bradbury, F A Whalley, J E Dyson, H Binns, W I Haigh, F J Bareham, J F W Newton
(Front row): F S Hudson, E Akroyd, J I Hopton, H Blackburn, Headmaster, L C Ash, R Addy, H Gledhill, T C Calloway

By 1950, with the increase in the birth rate, it became clear that Huddersfield required more grammar school places, and the retention of a two-stream grammar school at Almondbury was assured – at least for the time being.

It was at this time of controversy that John

Gerald Dobson: 'the knight in shining armour'

Baldwin retired. His deep love of Almondbury was ever apparent and found expression in his strong advocacy of the retention of its grammar school. He was ever vigilant in the defence of its traditions. The three years of his headship came as a fitting climax to his career. He had graced the chair with modesty and dignity. A composed, humane man, his term of office had been intrinsically true to the heritage of the past.

An interlude

Baldwin was succeeded by Horace Moore, formerly Senior Modern Language Master at St Peter's School, York. He was 48 years of age and had had wide experience in various grammar schools. He stayed only three years before returning to another headship in York.

During his time he strengthened the School in many ways. At St Peter's, the house system had been the keystone of corporate life and Moore sought to give the houses something more than distinguished names. He appointed housemasters; houses assembled each morning in house groups; boys dined in houses. Pastoral care within houses became more immediate and meaningful than hitherto. Boys across age groups shared many activities, and thereby a more significant and influential corporate life developed within houses.

School societies which had been a strong feature in the Taylor Dyson and Baldwin eras were further strengthened, and better facilities and resources were put at their disposal. A notable newcomer to the social scene was a junior version of the Jacobean Society called the Jak Society, named in commemoration of the School's forebears John and Arthur Kaye.

Education was central to the thinking of the post-war political revolution. Without its development the welfare state would have been on rocky foundations. There had been much pre-war neglect, not least in Huddersfield. National reforms were taking place, and Moore's tenure was one of adaptation.

A major challenge came in 1951 when a new system of examination was put in place. The former School Certificate and Higher School Certificate were replaced by the General Certificate of Education at Ordinary, Advanced and Scholarship levels. 'O levels', which approximated to the 'Credit' level of the old School Certificate, would be taken in as many subjects as the candidate was deemed to be ready. The other two levels were similar to the Higher School Certificate 'Principal' level.

The new examinations presented a tougher challenge. One of the hopes was that Sixth Forms would offer a less restricted curriculum than hitherto, but this was difficult to bring about. At Almondbury, there was much to be done before a better balance between Science and Arts could be achieved. For example, in 1950, of the 16 successful Higher School Certificate candidates only three were Arts students.

Moore's aspirations and their implicit challenges were strengthened by a combination of the 'old firm' and the 'new firm' in the staff room. Blackburn, Ash, Hopton, Akroyd, Haigh, Addy and Gledhill still soldiered on, and were reinforced by the return of Fred Hudson (from air force duty in Canada) and Thomas Calloway. New faces appeared, notably historian Francis Bareham and mathe-matician George Beach, both of whom were outstanding acquisitions and were to become devoted Almondburians.

During Moore's short stay he renewed the School despite murmuring in the wings. It

HEADMASTER
FACTFILE
1608-2008

NAME	Horace Vessey Moore
DATE OF APPOINTMENT	1948
DATE OF DEPARTURE	1951
DEGREE	MA
UNIVERSITY	Sheffield
LIFE IN BRIEF	Horace Moore, a graduate in Modern Languages, came to Almondbury at the age of 40 after eight years as Senior Modern Language Master at a public school, St Peter's, in York.

21

He did much to formalise the House system at King James's, introducing the concept of House masters and regular House assemblies. He also encouraged the setting up of a number of new clubs and societies devoted to topics ranging from model railways to music.

Educationally, he was responsible for easing the School's passage from the old system of School Certificate examinations into the new General Certificate of Education, introduced in 1951.

may well have been anxieties about the School's future that hastened his departure. Nevertheless he brought vigour and originality to his task. He had made a worthy contribution to the wellbeing of the School; its progress was an unanswerable riposte to the doubters elsewhere.

A UNIQUE OCCASION

One November evening in 1951 the 'Big' was packed. The occasion was the annual dinner of the Old Almondburians' Society. On the high table there was a

Horace Moore and his successor Harry Taylor were both keen to encourage activities outside the classroom. Chess had long been established at the School and it was stimulated further by the arrival of George Beach in 1949. In this 1953 photograph, George Beach looks on as his brother John Beach – a highly talented player who formed the Liverpool Chess Congress – played 50 boys from Huddersfield schools simultaneously in the Library. He won 38, drew 8 and lost 4 – all against players from King James's (Carl Goldsmith, Zarco Gakovic, Geoff Heeson and Robert Lee)

remarkable gathering of four headmasters. Taylor Dyson had made the journey from Christchurch; Horace Moore had returned from York; John Baldwin, ever present for so many years, his loyalty undimmed; and –

It was a night when the sense of being a part of historical continuity was intensified

the focus of many eyes – the recently appointed Harry Taylor. It was a night of reunion, a night of remembrance of absent friends, and for many – including myself – a night when the sense of being part of a historical continuity was intensified.

There were many speeches that night, two of which reamin in the memory. First, heralded by a great ovation, was a typically eloquent and emotional one by Taylor Dyson. It contained much humour as always and was a reminder of his unerring leadership of the School and his devotion to its traditions and welfare.

Be wide awake, be determined that the School retains the grammar school status on the present site. We don't want half measures. Beware of lukewarm friends who will say this and that. The idea of transferring the name to another school in another part of the town is anathema. Don't tolerate it for a moment.

He reminded all of us of the difficulties of articulating the intangible which permeated the history of the School and how its value, and indeed its values, would always be elusive to the perceptions of those who could only measure the immediate. It was a plea for vigilance, but also one of reassurance.

A pause … and then Harry Taylor made his debut. He had been appointed only a few months earlier. A new voice, yet from the outset it resonated confidence and an affinity with the School, the village and the Old Almondburians, as if he had found his destiny. He spoke with a distinctive brand of oratory and humour, his timing and composure matching the inspiration of his wit. He was given a great reception. As one Old Almondburian commented long afterwards:

He seemed at first sight and on first hearing so clearly an

Almondburian – appointing him was the best thing the Borough ever did for the School.

During the evening a memorial commemorating those Old Boys who had lost their lives during the Second World War was presented to the School. It took the form of a book containing the names of the 35 who had fallen and also of an oak bookcase made by the renowned northern craftsman Robert Thompson of Kilburn. Thus ended an evening of many mixed emotions.

So clearly an Almondburian

It is now over 40 years since I wrote my 'History of King James's Grammar School. During that time the School has known many changes, related elsewhere in this book by Dave Bush who served for some 35 years under four headmasters and became deputy head in 1972. Particularly memorable for him were those years when he was 'bound apprentice' to Harry Taylor.

If Harry had been awarded a peerage, I am sure he would have become 'Lord Taylor of St Helen's Gate.' He and his wife

HEADMASTER FACTFILE 1608-2008

NAME	Harry Taylor
DATE OF APPOINTMENT	1951
DATE OF DEPARTURE	1973
DEGREE	MA
UNIVERSITY	St John's College, Oxford
LIFE IN BRIEF	Harry Taylor was a man of many talents. His degree was in Modern History but he subsequently added to his qualifications by becoming a member of the Middle Temple and gaining the degree of Barrister of Law.

22

He fostered a close bond with the Old Almondburians' Society, which brought its own reward with the development of the Taylor Dyson Local History Library, the new cricket pavilion, and the vastly increased number of school prizes and trophies during his time as headmaster.

The School scaled new heights during these years. An inspired leader, he retired – to his sadness – at a time when the School's future was deeply uncertain because of national educational changes.

Jessica lived there, a mere stone's throw from the site of 'the chapel of old tyme'; each and every day, rain or shine, he walked down to the School which was as much a part of him as he was of it. The first twelve years of his stewardship are related in my book. He was the last of the Grammar School heads at Almondbury and many have – and will – testify to the fact that he ranks with the greatest. It would therefore be remiss of me not to mention here a few of my own impressions of him.

When in 1962 I broached the idea of writing a history of the School in succession to the one written by Taylor

Dyson in 1926, Harry was wary. 'Who is this chap? What's he up to? What has he done?' he mused. One summer day we met at the School. There was an instant rapport. Puffing away at his pipe, he asked me if I knew the latest score from Headingley. We, like most cricketing buffs, lamented the passing of those days when Yorkshire were supreme and Herbert Sutcliffe scored 'a century a week.' He spoke with pride of the School and his privilege to be

Harry Taylor presented his first report as Headmaster at Speech Day in Huddersfield Town Hall on 10th March 1952 when the guest speaker was Sir Harold Himsworth. He said that the School was 'not a little proud' that both the guest speaker and the chairman, Alderman J L Dawson, both came from the ranks of the Old Almondburians

part of it. He gave me his approval! During the writing of the history, Harry read each and every chapter, and gave me wise counsel and encouragement. He became my friend. Indeed, whenever he was looking for a promising recruit to his staff he would ring me at the university and I like to think that I provided him with several 'winners'. Certainly they enjoyed their days at the School.

Harry was the last of a line. I have met them all. Perhaps not 'one Mr Smyth' who will always remain a mystery. But I know the rest. I have heard Farrand proclaiming his Royalist sympathies; I have met Sedgewick in his hayfield; I have journeyed with Sam Brooke as he rode past Woodsome on his way to his Flockton chapelry; I have walked with Easther and Nowell up the road to Farnley Cock. I have had a drink with Marshall in the Woolpack; I have rubbed shoulders with Crump at the Woodsome Hall pageant; and in reality I have listened with wonder as Taylor Dyson electrified many an assembly with his oratory.

And I have met Harry. I would have liked to have seen him playing cricket. I would have liked to have been present on those auspicious occasions when in assembly, as a trustee of Nettleton's Charity, he received from himself a red rose in keeping with the terms of the endowment in 1620. I would have liked to have thanked him for his transcription of the Almondbury parish registers which illuminated the history of the village in such a vivid and far-reaching way.

I used to meet Harry at Old Almondburian dinners and, at his kind invitation, I spoke at Speech Day in 1964. Over the years I had many interesting letters from him. We kept in touch.

In 1964, I concluded my narrative of his headship to that date thus:

Not a little of the School's present position is attributable to the wisdom and balanced judgement of the present headmaster. A mature and tolerant man, he has proved himself as a scholar and as a leader. He is above all an Almondburian in the best traditions of all those who have given of their talents to ensure the continuity and high standing of the School. He wears the mantle with dignity: long may he do so.

Harry's two sons Richard and Andrew both attended King James's. Their unique memories of Harry as headmaster and father, which follow, make fascinating reading.

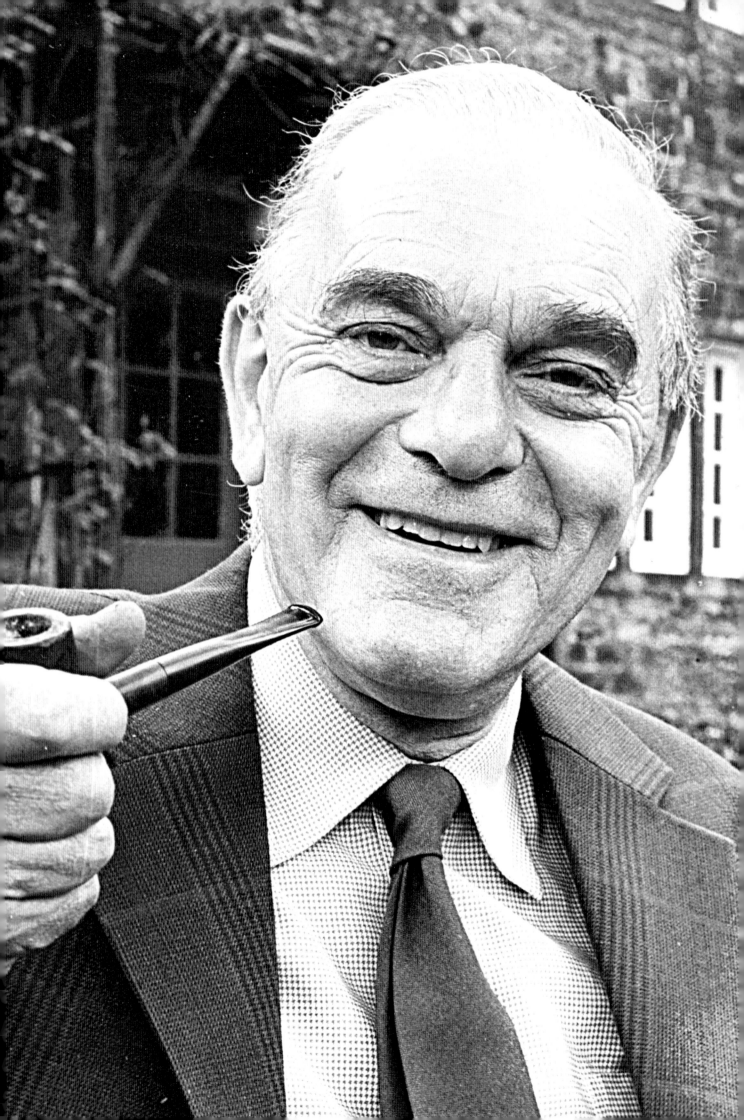

The Harry Taylor years

Harry Taylor was the highly respected headmaster from 1951 - 1973. His two sons, who attended the School in his time, remember him as 'the Gaffer' - and as a father

RICHARD TAYLOR (1954 - 62)

LIKE MOST YOUNG PEOPLE, I had various disagreements with my father, and again, as in most of these situations, he usually won and was usually right. I did, however, win one very important argument at the tender age of ten. I had passed the 11+ examination and my parents, in discussion with me, had to decide if they wanted me to attend Almondbury Grammar School (as it was then known) or Huddersfield College. My father felt that to have his son as a boy at the School might cause problems for the boy, the Headmaster/father, the staff and other pupils. The boy's heart was set on Almondbury, and the father gave in. Later he was to praise my persistence which enabled us to enjoy a wonderful, shared experience so deep that it is hard to quantify to those without it. Perhaps he had always wanted me to go to the School, but felt that he had to give me the chance to say no.

My father became Headmaster of Almondbury Grammar School in 1951. He spoke at the Old Almondburians' Dinner in November of that year (when the War Memorial Bookcase was dedicated), and one Old Almondburian reported that 'he seemed at first sight and on first hearing so clearly an Almondburian'. Rather more cheesily, the School magazine referred to him as 'a unique present from Doncaster Grammar School' – but it *was* the Christmas edition!

As recorded elsewhere in this book, in 1952 a party of boys visiting an exhibition of documents at the Yorkshire Archaeological Society 'rediscovered' the School Charter and Statutes. The Charter's date was confirmed as 1608 (not 1609 as previously thought) and the valuable documents returned to their home at School, to the delight of the new Headmaster. (It is, perhaps, no coincidence, that as I look through my father's handwritten

My father thought that to have his son as a boy at the School might cause problems

book of 'Prayers for Morning Assembly', the first two prayers are taken from the Statutes: '... bestow on every one of us a discerning spirit, a sound judgement and an honest and good heart ... ').

Perhaps the discovery of the Charter helped to stir thoughts on the School's heritage, as in 1955 the undistinguished AGS monogram was replaced by the distinctive royal coat of arms, still displayed on School clothing. I recall my father making enquiries about registering the coat of arms with the College of Heralds, but it proved to be too expensive!

Having secured the coat of arms, my father now went after the name. It took some time, but a letter from the Home Office of 27 March, 1959 stated that 'Her Majesty has been graciously pleased to command that the Almondbury Grammar School shall be known as "King James's Grammar School" '.

The reintroduction of the coat of arms and the ancient name added lustre to a

Richard Taylor is currently, with Paul Balderstone, joint Chairman of the Old Almondburians' Society. He spent eight happy years at King James's before gaining an Honours Degree in Modern History and a Diploma in Education at St. Edmund Hall, Oxford. He undertook a Diploma in Physical Education and subsequently taught at Wakefield College where he spent 23 years as Head of Leisure, Recreation & Sport. Richard retired in 1995 and fills many hours as Chief Examiner/Lead Verifier with various examination boards. He is still a playing member of the MCC and enjoys watching his four sons playing a very wide range of sports at various levels.

school which was rapidly carving out a reputation for itself.

The celebrations to mark the 350th Anniversary of the Charter in 1958 were a highpoint in my time at School, and I know they were for my father. The previous year, the School Fair had raised £1,000 which was used as the basis for the construction of the cricket pavilion to mark the Anniversary. It is a sobering thought, in these days of corporate sponsorship, that the money was raised from sheer hard work by staff, students, old boys and parents. I recall my mother running sewing evenings with the staff wives – for example, with Mrs. Baldwin, wife of the former Head, crippled with arthritis, doing her crocheting – and Mrs. Billington, a parent, running a stall selling toilet soaps.

Thursday, June 5th, 1958, was the day chosen to open the new Pavilion. It has suffered in the ensuing 50 years, but then it was a marvellous facility to grace the beautiful cricket field at Arkenley – a field which my father had had extended by the tipping of household rubbish in the lower half, and where people still occasionally dig in the banking for old bottles.

I remember the day as warm and sunny (as did the scorer, David Billington, writing in the School magazine) and it was one of those wonderful days when the whole School appeared around the cricket field. A strong Headmaster's XI, including Billy Sutcliffe (recently captain of Yorkshire) and Mel Ryan (Yorkshire) drew the cricket match with an Old Almondburians' XI, though they had the best of the game. Sutcliffe, I remem-

ber, scored 87 in a fine exhibition of batting, and Ryan took 4 wickets. At 3 pm the Countess of Scarborough arrived and, having driven around the ground, declared the Pavilion open in the presence of Alderman J L Dawson, an Old Almondburian who was chairman of the Governors for much of my father's time, and Cllr

Mr Oddy of Oddy's Ices always provided free ice creams for the Staff, despite the boys being the ones using the energy

Kenneth Brooke, Chairman of the Old Almondburians' Society whose grandsons currently turn out for the Old Almondburians' Cricket Club. As a further example of the spirit of 'self-help' that existed in those days, Cllr Brooke and a few of his fellow Old Almondburians had only completed the painting of the pavilion a few weeks before, having discovered to their concern that the money had run out with £200 still needed.

The celebrations for the 350th Anniversary concluded in November with an Old Almondburians' Dinner in Huddersfield Town Hall, graced by the Mayor and Sir Harold Himsworth, who was at one time physician to the Queen. This grand occasion provided a fitting climax to the year.

Sport was always high on the agenda at King James's. The Headmaster's XI v the School, and the Staff v the Prefects cricket matches were watched by the whole School each summer. Sports Day was another afternoon out of the classroom for everybody, with fine performances on the rather quaint 220 yard [198 m] circular grass track. On these occasions, Mr Oddy of Oddy's Ices always provided free ice creams for the Staff, despite the boys being the ones using the energy!

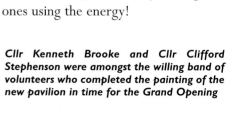

Cllr Kenneth Brooke and Cllr Clifford Stephenson were amongst the willing band of volunteers who completed the painting of the new pavilion in time for the Grand Opening

Albert Makinson's production of 'Tobias and the Angel' in March 1958.
H E Taylor, P M Westerby, R I Mallinson,
C G Mallinson (seated), W M Thornton (recumbent), R N Sykes, P Swinden, J Dobson

Season 1958/59 was a golden one for the Football XI captained by George Law, when 16 games were won. Two highlights spring to mind. On 20th January, the School played Normanton Grammar School, with the whole School watching. These were the only two unbeaten schools in Yorkshire and I remember the game as a glorious draw: the records show a 3-2 defeat for King James's! At the end of the season, the team won the Yorkshire Grammar Schools seven-a-side competition at Harrogate, a result made sweeter by a thrashing for Huddersfield New College on the way to the title. On their return to School the team managed to sneak the result and the trophy into that night's School performance of *Alice in Wonderland*.

Many sporting honours were achieved, perhaps motivated by Old Almondburian Derek Ibbotson's achievements of a Bronze Medal in the Melbourne Olympic Games and his World Mile Record in 1957 (the impressive photograph hangs in the Pavilion). George Law and Richard ('Charlie') Hall represented Yorkshire at football, Peter Westerby did so at cricket, and Allen Ross proved to be a shot putter of national repute, and later our first Cambridge 'Blue'. He also, incidentally, nearly killed his mother on Sports Day by putting the shot a prodigious distance!

Sport was not all, however. Drama productions were a highlight each year, including various Shakespearean productions, *Tobias and the Angel* and – as mentioned earlier – *Alice in Wonderland*. The part of Alice was so big that two Alices were used, one before and the other after the interval! Almost as exciting as the productions was the rather eccentric portable stage erected each year in the gymasium.

Music, and the School Orchestra under George Beach, added to the mix, especially on Speech Days in the Town Hall, where Harry Gledhill used to challenge the School to move the chandeliers with the volume of the singing of the School Song.

The School Scout Troop dated from 1955 under the leadership of Bill Rennison and Jim Toomey, and made an excellent addition to the activities on offer.

Academic successes increased, with Open and Borough Scholarships, many University places and an increase in Oxbridge entries. Some high achievers, such as Sir Harold Himsworth and Professor Ben Wortley (Professor of Jurisprudence and International Law at Manchester University) returned to inspire on Speech Days. Yet of equal importance to my father and his team were those who did not reach the highest academic levels, but who made the most of their talents and gained worthy successes in the professions and business. Many of them were to prove stalwarts of the Old Almondburians' Society.

An expanding School requires extra buildings, and the new biology laboratory and staffroom were added in

He boasted that he had never appointed anyone who refused Saturday games duty

1957. Six years later, the Countess of Dartmouth came to open further extensions.

My father's 'team' at Almondbury was a remarkable one. He once proudly boasted that he had never appointed anyone who refused Saturday games duty (he rarely missed Saturday matches, winter or summer, himself). The talents of those he inherited and those he appointed were many and varied.

For his first two years, Leonard Ash served as Deputy Head before retiring in 1953. (As relaxation, the two of them and their wives enjoyed a game of Ludo!). Fred Hudson became Deputy in 1953 and was to hold the post until both he and Harry retired in 1973. It was a happy and fruitful partnership. I was particularly grateful to Fred for dealing with my university entrance as Harry, quite rightly, felt he should not be involved.

There were many other talented staff, but two of my father's appointees stand out to me, and I know they did to him. In 1959 Jack Taylor arrived to teach Biology and was to remain at King James's for the rest of his long and distinguished career. As a local cricketer of note, he had of course a distinct advantage in interview with my father. In 1960, in Jim Toomey's absence through illness, my father asked Leeds University (helpfully, the Professor of Classics had been at Manchester with my mother!) to send an able classics student as he would have to take on virtually a full timetable. Enter Dave Bush, who was to spend his whole teaching life at Almondbury and make a massive contribution to the lives of his pupils. These two 'giants' have carried forward and enhanced the achievements of the Harry Taylor years.

In 1962 I finally left after eight very happy years at King James's, to be followed, 12 months later, by a younger brother. I don't think my father's forebodings about having a son in the School were realised, and neither did he. He once said that he knew the pupils of my year and my brother's year better than any, because he met so many of them socially. I achieved most of what I wanted at School; Cricket Captain and Jacobean Chairman were highlights, but Head Boy, we both recognised, was never a possibility even if I had had the talent. The Staff and my peers were superb in accepting me as just another boy – as we both wanted.

Two incidents in the second form (age 12) probably helped me to avoid future difficulties. My Form Master, Albert Makinson, took me on one side, when I had perhaps become a little cocky, and told me quite clearly that I was certainly nothing special and to behave accordingly. On another occasion I was caned by my father (sorry, by the Headmaster!) for fighting with a form mate, David Quarmby, who was later to become Head Boy. We were taken to the Study by a member of staff (who shall remain nameless), and received our beatings. Years later my father told me it was not a caning offence, but he was being tested out by the member of staff. That may be so, but at the time the incident gave me food for thought (and a degree of pain) and it probably helped my 'street cred' at School. (Incidentally, he never told my mother, and I've never told David Quarmby that it was not a caning offence).

I regarded my father at home as father, friend and Headmaster in that order. At School, he was Headmaster, and, latterly friend. In eight years I never once walked down the hill to School with him, nor returned up the hill back home in his company. I loved being at his School and, biased as I am, I respected and rejoiced in his achievements as Headmaster. I was privileged to see many things from two sides, and I'm sure this helped in my own career.

He wrote somewhere that history should never be a burden, but each generation adds something to the life of a school. I'm sure he added immeasurably to King James's Grammar School. ◗

ANDREW TAYLOR (1963 - 70)

SEPTEMBER 1963, and a small boy is hurrying desperately along the school corridor, at the bottom of the stairs leading up to Dorm 2. The shiny new leather satchel banging on his hip, the bright yellow blazer badge, and the well-scrubbed knees you can see below his grey shorts give him away as a new boy. And so does his panic.

No running in the school corridors, of course – but he is late for French in the Small, and he scampers head-down, top speed, around the corner by the Library …

Thump! He collides with a large, portly figure in a pale grey suit walking the other way, and looks up in abject

Andrew Taylor left King James's Grammar School, as it then was, in 1970, having managed – unlike his pugilistic brother – to get through his time there without being caned by the Headmaster. After a career in journalism which started with the *Yorkshire Evening Post* and ended with the BBC, by way of the Press Association and the *Daily Express,* he travelled to the Middle East in 1988 to work for Dubai Television. While he was there, he started writing books about the Gulf and the Arab world, and continued writing when he returned to England in 1993. He claims that he never quite managed to find what his father used to call a 'proper job'.

horror. Luckily, the large figure is smiling jovially — laughing, even. 'Hello, young man! And where are you going?'

'Oh my God! The Gaffer!' (That bit was silent). 'French, Sir. Er – sorry, Sir. Morning, Sir! Umm! Er …' And he scampers off, like a runaway hamster looking for a hole to hide in.

Well, it was me, of course, suddenly facing the new

' … you didn't mess with his Grammar School boys if you knew what was good for you'

reality that my father had changed into the Gaffer on his five minute walk down the hill from home. Luckily for me, my brother had been at school for eight years, and had set the ground rules. Whatever happens, he's always the Headmaster at school, never Dad. He was also, incidentally, on that day when I nearly knocked him flying, a year or so younger than I am now, which seems somehow odd.

But of course, he was both – the distant, awe-inspiring figure who made that long, dignified walk into assembly always somehow dimly reminiscent of the occasionally stern, always demanding, but unfailingly supportive man I knew from home.

Just as I knew as I grew up that he was always on my side, so you didn't mess with his Grammar School boys if you knew what was good for you. An Almondbury resident telephoned once to complain that boys were running past her front door on their cross-countries: the Headmaster listened politely, and then firmly reminded her that his boys had as much right to use the road as anyone else. Thank you and good-bye.

Another complaint came about the conduct of the end-of-school bus queues in the village. Again, he listened in well-mannered silence — and over the next few days, completely unknown to me or anybody else, he left school early to go and sit quietly in an upstairs room in the baker's shop which overlooked the bus stop. And then he phoned back, to say that he had been watching the boys, and they had behaved impeccably. End of conversation. Don't mess with my boys.

In turn, there were aspects of the schoolmaster about him at home. For instance, we had long and passionate conversations about politics as I grew up, but I never knew for sure which way he voted. It was the sort of thing teachers didn't tell you in those days — you were expected to make your own mind up. I know he felt cheated by the Labour Party, because he saw grammar schools as a way out for bright boys from poor backgrounds, and he thought a Labour government should have supported him, instead of trying to destroy his school – but that feeling was matched by his contempt (my word, not his: I can't imagine him being so rude) for the local Conservative politicians who finished off what Labour had started. You didn't need to agree with his point of view to feel for his sense of betrayal.

And long hair, of course. Forty years later, I still have a sinking feeling of defeat whenever I go for a hair cut, after all those years as a teenager when I tried unsuccessfully to put off the evil day by disguising the fact that my hair was beginning to curl over my collar, or that my adolescent sideburns were edging ambitiously down the side of my face. The man who would pull boys out of assembly and send them up to the village barber's with five shillings of

Harry Taylor with his 'team' in 1967.
Back row: Y M Etchevest,
L Mallinson, R Wearing, R Beever,
S Wroe, J E Kenyon, M P James,
Mrs H M Hebblethwaite, C Hindley,
A C Brown, C H Gill, K L W Ireland,
R G Walker.
Front row: W Western, J P Toomey,
G W Chapman, D A Bush,
F S Hudson, Harry Taylor, J Taylor,
P H Heywood, F J Bareham,
G L Beach, W I Haigh

his own money in their pocket was hardly going to let his own son grow his hair. It was a peculiar blind spot that he had: 'What sportsman, what professional footballer has ever gone onto the field with long hair?' he asked indignantly in assembly one morning. 'Well, actually, Dad, quite a few – George Best, for a start …' Not the sort of thing you could say to the Head.

On the other hand, he could give ground graciously when he had to. He hated motorcycles with a passion – there was a twelve month spell when I was sixteen when I didn't speak a sentence at home which didn't have the word 'motorbike' in it, although I think I knew all along that it was never going to happen for me. He tried desperately to persuade those boys at school who did have motorbikes not to come to school on them – but when he failed, he arranged with the landlord at the Woolpack in the village for them to use his car-park. (I still go cold imagining what would have happened if he had ever found out about those lunchtimes when I was in the Fifth Form, riding on my friends' bikes at madcap speeds down Farnley Line).

The Scout Troop formed a Guard of Honour at the opening of the new cricket pavilion by the Countess of Scarborough in 1958. Harry Taylor was a staunch supporter of scouting – and cricket – at the School

Or there was a sixth form current affairs lesson where he was being harangued about a spate of university sit-ins and the iniquity of the secret political files that were apparently kept on students. (People cared about these things in those days.) He dipped in his pocket, pulled out his bunch of keys, and tossed them across the table. 'Go and look for yourself,' he said casually. Of course, the boy didn't – game, set and match to the Gaffer.

But there was nothing casual about his attitude to his job: it was a responsibility that was always with him. Not long before I left, there were some boys who had been caught stealing sweets in Almondbury. Being 18, and therefore knowing everything, I took it upon myself to remind him that they probably had pretty difficult home backgrounds, and to suggest that perhaps he ought to let them off with a warning. 'It's all right for you to say that,' he said, with just a trace of bitterness at my failure to see his position. 'You don't have any responsibility. You don't have to do anything – but what message will it give them if I don't punish them? What I do or don't do might affect whether they do this again in the future, and get themselves into more trouble.' I think it's fair to assume that he didn't treat them leniently.

He hadn't always meant to spend his whole career at King James's, which was his first headship. He was only 41, and I think the original plan was to stay for a while, and then move on to a bigger school, and clamber a bit further up the ladder. But he told me once that, after a couple of years, he'd been climbing the hill to the Woolpack one night, and he'd stopped and looked back at St Helen's Gate, and thought about the village of Almondbury, about King James's and its history, about the people he was working with there, and about the long list of headmasters before him, and he realised that in every way he was in the place where he wanted to spend the rest of his life – which, I can see now, doesn't seem like a bad definition of success.

Some of the things he believed in seem old fashioned now – but as it's more than thirty years since he retired, it would be odd if they didn't. Some, like the short back-and-sides, seemed old fashioned even then. But all the different stories people tell about him, all the things I remember about him at school and at home, add up to a man who was wise, and kind, and funny, and determined. A man who cared about cricket, and liked a beer, and grew chrysanthemums, and would sit up late at night reading poetry. A much more rounded figure, maybe, than most people ever saw at school.

And so it still seems odd when speakers at Old Almondburians' dinners and other functions sometimes say a few words about Harry Taylor the headmaster. Of course I'm proud when I hear them say what a fine head he was – but there is always just a little part of me that thinks to myself, 'You don't know the half of it.' ◼

The Royal Charter returns to its home at King James's

ROGER DOWLING tells the strange story of the Charter's 'disappearance' and its eventual chance rediscovery in 1952 by members of the School's Surveying Society

'THE ORIGINAL LETTERS PATENT do not exist', recorded Taylor Dyson in his classic *Almondbury and its Ancient School* of 1926, echoing the words of Canon Hulbert's earlier *Annals of the Church and Parish of Almondbury*. But they were both wrong: the Letters Patent ('the Charter') in fact lay, undisturbed over many years, in a strong box at the unlikely location of Denby Grange Colliery just a few miles away on the road to

Wakefield. So how did the School come to be parted from its own Charter? And why did it require the services of the School's Surveying Society to reunite it with the School on 6th April 1954?

It all started with a planned visit by members of the Society, led by Geography master Fred Hudson, to a local history exhibition being organised by the Yorkshire Archaeological Society in Leeds. Hudson was

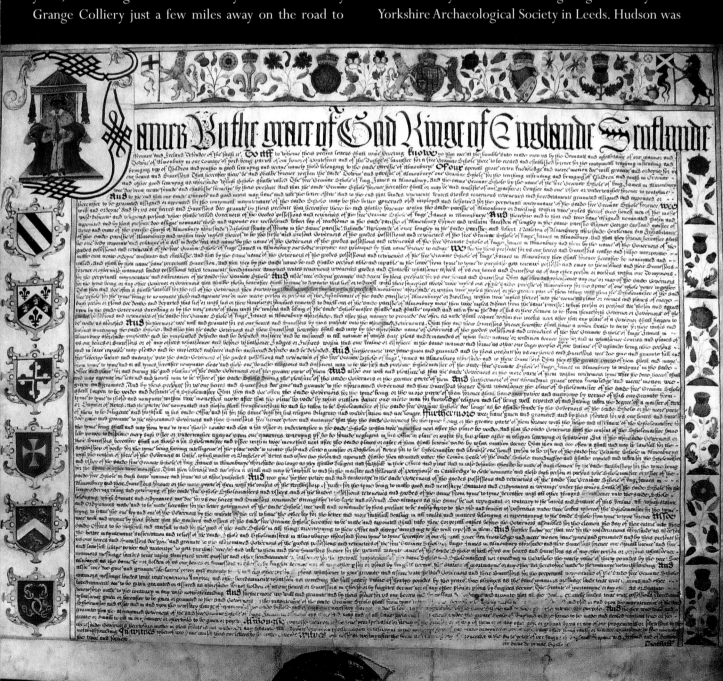

himself a keen historian and amateur archaeologist, and had often involved pupils in digs at Castle Hill and elswhere in the district.

Quite by chance, a few days before the exhibition someone mentioned to Allan Dobson, a member of the Surveying Society, that the *Yorkshire Observer* had carried a preview which mentioned the intriguing fact that the exhibition included 'Court documents dating back to the 12th century, the foundation charter of Almondbury Grammar School bearing the seal of James I, and a collection of ancient pottery.' He recalls:

At the time I had no idea of the significance of the appearance of the Charter and didn't even bother to mention it to Fred Hudson.

When they arrived at the exhibition, on 6th May 1952, Allan Dobson and fellow surveyor Alan Sykes decided 'in no particular haste' to seek out the document. Their efforts were soon rewarded: there, in all its glory, was THE School Charter; not just an old copy but plainly the original parchment of 1608.

But even then it was a little while before that they thought to mention it to Fred Hudson, by this time

They rediscovered the Royal Charter: Michael Fawcett, David Anderson, Tommy Blackburn, John Earnshaw, Allan Dobson and Alan Sykes proudly pose with the Charter in Fenay Quad. Any thoughts of examining the 'ancient pottery' at the Leeds exhibition were quickly abandoned

happily investigating the ancient pottery. Allan Dobson continues:

I asked 'Sir' if he had seen the Charter yet, and I recall that he seemed not to realise at first that the Charter was that of the School. Fred Hudson and I were in a state of some excitement at that stage — mine was one of bewilderment and Fred's one of disbelief!

Still at first unconvinced, Fred Hudson joined Dobson, Sykes and the other boys as they peered at the magnificent document, complete with massive King James seal, that had been thought lost for centuries. But now, at last, it was found!

David Anderson, another of the six pupils who was present on that fateful day in 1952, gives his account:

Soapy Hudson was very keen on history and archaeology. When we heard that there was the opportunity to participate in a special trip to an exhibition in Leeds a number of us were keen to go along. We had only been there about ten minutes or so and then someone

'Fred Hudson and I were in a state of some excitement at that stage ...'

broke the news that our school charter was on display. I rushed over to find Allan Dobson and Soapy looking with disbelief at this splendid document. I can't remember any of us bothering to look at anything else that afternoon!

Astonishingly, the Archaeological Society's archivist, Miss Foster, was completely unaware that the School did not know that the Society had the Charter in safe keeping. Moreover, 'if the School was interested', the Society also had the ancient Statutes, dating back to 1700. It was an occasion of high drama and excitement.

But how had the Yorkshire Archeological Society acquired these priceless documents? And how did Denby Grange Colliery become involved? Subsequent research by Fred Hudson, and Gerald Hinchliffe, provided the answer.

As has been recorded elsewhere is this book, the Kaye

The Statutes were also found to be safely in the custody of the Yorkshire Archaeological Society. Drawn up between 1695 and 1700, during the headship of Rev Abraham Walker, they comprised three rolls of parchment together measuring over 3m (10ft) in length

family of Woodsome Hall have had a long association with King James's School, dating right back to the rebuilding of the ancient chantry school by John and Arthur Kaye in 1547. The School Charter, which carried the name of Robert Kaye, was a document of which the family was understandably proud, and it seems almost certain that it was stored safely in the family vaults at Woodsome rather than at the often cold and damp School a few miles away.

By 1679 the sole governor of the School was Sir John Kaye. He died in 1706, and his son Arthur 20 years later, at which point the Kaye title passed to Sir Arthur's nephew John Kaye of Denby Grange. John Kaye took the name of Sir John Lister-Kaye and was himself a governor of the School between 1734 and 1752.

In more recent times, Sir Kenelm Lister-Kaye succeeded to the baronetcy in 1931. He was a bachelor who was often away serving in the Army and the Royal Air Force, as a result of which Denby Grange – still with

Denby Grange and shown to Dr J W Walker, a Wakefield historian who was at that time President of the Yorkshire Archeological Society. (By a happy coincidence, this organisation had its origins in the Huddersfield Archeological and Topographical Society set up at Almondbury Grammar School in 1864 by Alfred Easther, John Nowell, Canon Hulbert and Thomas Brooke of Fenay Hall).

Recognising the importance of the find, Dr Walker offered to provide a safe custody alongside the other artefacts in the Yorkshire Archeological Society's collection, and accordingly the Charter and Statutes were handed over to the Society in October 1946. Curiously, no-one seemed to have thought about notifying the School.

And so it was that a further six years elapsed before a chance visit to an exhibition in Leeds led to the School being reunited with its beloved documents. Amicable arrangements were immediately made with the Yorkshire Archeological Society for the Charter and Statutes to made available to the School on 'permanent loan', and an Old Almondburian, Kenneth Brooke, provided a magnificent display cabinet in which the Charter could be viewed under glass. The formal handover ceremony took place at the School on 6th April 1954, in the presence of the chairman of the governors (Alderman J L Dawson), the Mayor of Huddersfield (Coun W Mallinson), the Town Clerk (Harry Bann) and the Vicar of Almondbury (Canon Bellman). ◗

its strong box containing both the Charter (and subsequently the Statutes) – was often unoccupied. Sir Kenelm therefore decided that the valuable documents would be safer in the strong room at the nearby family-owned Denby Grange colliery.

Just before it was nationalised after the Second World War, the agent to the Denby Grange Estate, Mr J E Kilburn, was given the task of clearing out the colliery premises and to his surprise discovered the Charter and Statutes in a strong box. They were returned hastily to

---

● *The Charter and Statutes are now with the West Yorkshire Archive Service at Kirklees Central Library*

Grammar to comprehensive: the years of change

King James's has always been in a state of constant evolution. But no changes have been as profound as those of the past 50 years, recalled here by DAVE BUSH

'**I**T NEVER HAPPENED in the Grammar School days' became a stock introduction to an exchange between Doreen Hinchliffe and me whenever certain difficult situations arose during King James's days as a Comprehensive. Mrs Hinchliffe served as School Secretary for 25 years from 1966 to 1991. I believe the expression was first used when the caretaker was called to the girls' toilets to repair the Tampax machine which had become jammed with a coin.

I had first made my way down St. Helen's Gate in November 1960 as a student teacher. Even my second practice at Pudsey Grammar had a King James's connection for it was under the supervision of one Fred Bungeroth, ('Hoppit'), previously Head of French at King James's. I returned to the school for some temporary teaching in the Summer Term and took up a permanent post in September 1961. I had undergone an interview during which I was asked by one councillor my opinion on capital punishment in schools. I remained at King James's in various capacities until my retirement in July 1996. With sixty years service between us, 'Mrs H' and I had some grounds for making comparisons but subsequent observations are very much a personal perspective.

Gerald Hinchliffe's erudite and inspirational *History of King James's School in Almondbury* concludes with an idyllic description of the old Schoolhouse and garden. Yet the rabbits which had just frisked across the grass as he finished his book were soon to be alarmed by the shots of change fired from the Local Education Authority offices in Kirkgate and which echoed across the Farnley Valley. Grammar Schools were deemed outdated;

Comprehensives were the modern way to educate. Despite protest groups being formed and personal approaches to the then Minister for Education, Margaret Thatcher, King James's along with Huddersfield's other grammar schools had to close. September 1972 saw the last of the Grammar School intake. But the LEA had a problem. What educational use could be found for such an historic and glorious site? Their solution was to establish King James's Sixth Form College, an evolution which had already befallen Greenhead and New College. Along with their male counterparts, the first girls in 366 years entered the portals – or the Old Kitchen Entrance – in September 1974.

However, it soon became apparent that Huddersfield could not sustain three colleges, and King James's size and situation worked against it. A further change was needed! Demographic shifts had seen a rapid increase in housing in areas such as Kirkheaton and Lepton. These villages had Middle Schools catering for pupils from 9 to 13. King James's could provide the requisite places for children between 13 and 18. While other schools in the town added 'High' to their name, King James's became, thankfully, simply 'King James's School'. It was to provide mixed comprehensive education for pupils aged 13-

Dave Bush was born in Billingborough, South Lincs. After studying at the University of Leeds, where he was awarded an honours degree in languages and met his future wife Margaret, he spent his entire teaching career at King James's. Beginning in 1961 as a junior Latin, French and English teacher under such 'giants' as Jim Toomey, Dick Addy and Frank Anderson, he progressively became housemaster of Jessop, Head of Latin and eventually Deputy Headmaster. Between Harry Taylor's retirement and Alan Conley's arrival, he was Acting Headmaster; he describes the time spent sitting in Harry Taylor's chair as his most daunting but inspiring time at King James's. He retired in July 1996 and moved to South Wales.

The educational mutations of 1972 - 1990

THE VARIOUS CHANGES in the character of the School that occurred after 1972 were foreshadowed by the decision of Huddersfield Council in 1964 to reorganise the education system in the town 'on comprehensive lines', as they had been exhorted to do by the Government.

Working parties were set up to establish a comprehensive education scheme best suited to Huddersfield's needs and the outcome was a proposal (within the old Huddersfield County Borough area) to set up:

- 4 Primary Schools (age group 5 - 11)
- 18 Infants Schools (age group 5 - 7)
- 17 Junior Schools (age group 7 - 11)
- 8 Comprehensive Schools (age group 11 - 16)
- 3 Sixth From Colleges (age group 16 - 18/19)
(and the Technical College providing for the same age group).
- All schools were to be co-educational
- In addition, there would be a group of Catholic Schools

The proposals, as submitted to the then Secretary of State for Education, Margaret Thatcher, envisaged the change of the three local authority grammar schools – King James's (boys), New College (boys) and Greenhead (girls) – into three co-educational sixth form colleges.

In the event, following strong representations that King James's should remain as a grammar school, Mrs Thatcher took the view that there would be adequate sixth-form provision without King James's. However, the Council appealed against this decision on the grounds that the imminent introduction of the new education authority – Kirklees Metropolitan Council – would result in a larger catchment area; furthermore, the local population was likely to rise because of improved motorway communication links.

There was huge controversy at the time and many column-inches of debate ensued in the correspondence columns of *The Huddersfield Examiner*. After a long period of uncertainty, a meeting with Mrs Thatcher resulted in her performing an uncharacteristic U-turn and it was agreed that from 1974 King James's could, after all, become Huddersfield's third sixth-form college.

But there was yet a further twist to the story. Mrs Thatcher's initial judgement was vindicated when it was soon found that two sixth form colleges would, after all, largely serve the town's needs. In 1976 King James's took on a new role as a co-educational comprehensive, initially for the age group 13 - 18 and, from 1990, for the age group 11 - 16.

except the one w... ...would ha... ch... ...ames's Grammar School into a sixth form college. The indications are that two such colleges will be enough for Huddersfield's needs in the foreseeable future and that it would be undesirable, on educational grounds, to add a third. King James's will, therefore, remain unchanged when the authority begin - in September 1973 - to implement the other proposals which I have approved.

The Iron Lady has spoken - but what did she mean? This letter, written by Mrs Thatcher in 1972 when she was Secretary of State for Education, caused huge controversy: having turned down the LEA's proposal to convert King James's into a sixth form college, did she mean it should remain a grammar school? But the question became academic when, in due course, she relented.

18 drawn from the feeder schools at Kirkheaton, Lepton, Grange Moor and Flockton, although the latter eventually transferred to the Shelley pyramid. How ironic that a child living opposite the School gates could not cross the road to be educated!

September 1976 epitomises 'The Years of Change'. Imagine going into Assembly on the first day of the new school year. Ranged in front of the Head, Alan Conley, is a school which comprises the last of the Sixth Form College in the Upper Sixth (Year 13), no Lower Sixth (Year 12), the last of the two stream Grammar School boys in the fifth form (Year 11), no fourth form (Year 10) and the first 180 mixed ability boys and girls in the third form (Year 9). It is highly unlikely that this ludicrous situation has ever been replicated in any other institution in Britain.

Yet even this arrangement was to obtain only until July 1990. The pressures of wider choice of subjects, adult atmosphere and above all finance meant that small sixth forms such as the one in St. Helen's Gate were no longer viable. The indefensible cost of teaching groups of two or three was placing an unfair burden on Lower School class sizes. King James's lost its Sixth Form but it is interesting to note that all the other schools in Huddersfield and District, including Honley and Colne Valley, followed suit. Today only Shelley's remains. Middle Schools and Open Plan were now no longer in vogue. Cynicism is hard to keep at bay.

In September 1990 some 300

pupils became Years 7 and 8 (1st and 2nd forms for those who still cling to the old nomenclature) and King James's 11-16 School came into existence. One positive advantage of this change of age group was that local children could now join King James's and numbers were boosted by a steady increase in intake of children living in Almondbury, Dalton and Rawthorpe. The 11-16 status has now been retained for 17 years, a period of stability much appreciated and enjoyed by all those who have the welfare of this famous institution close to their hearts.

This, then, is an outline of the fundamental changes in school status over nearly 50 years. Of much more interest and importance is the effect those changes had on staff and pupils and on the environment in which they educated or were educated. Some could be described as the natural result of changes in educational thinking – grammar to comprehensive, for example – while others were necessitated by physical demands: the doubling in size of the school intake is an obvious one. The description of ancillary staff may seem a strange way to begin but it illustrates perfectly the points being made.

It is said that visitors to the school in the sixties not infrequently mistook the caretaker, Arthur Stockdale, for the Headmaster. Usually smartly attired Arthur had an authoritative air about him and took his holidays at a rather smart hotel in Lytham St Anne's. When asked his profession Arthur allegedly said he was 'in education'. Staff attended his house in Fenay Lane for pre-Christmas drinks and he accompanied school holiday parties to France. At this time the Lab assistant was

Visitors not infrequently mistook the caretaker for the Headmaster

'Raymond'. Nobody seemed to know his surname. On one occasion Raymond was asked to unblock a sink in the Chemistry Lab. This he did by unscrewing the waste pipe and placing a bucket beneath. When the said bucket was full, its contents were immediately poured down the sink and spread widely over the floor. In contrast the role of the modern caretaker or rather 'site manager' demands a wide range of handyman skills while at least one lab assistant has had a PhD. Another, a tall gentleman with swept back grey hair and immaculate long white lab coat – the pupils nicknamed him 'Doctor Death' – had held a managerial position in a recently closed textile mill. Arthur and Raymond belonged to a different era. In the present school they simply could not have coped.

Could Harry Taylor, considered by many to have been one of King James's finest heads, have coped? Highly unlikely, but then the question should not really be put for he too reflected a different era. He retired in July 1973, still the head of a small, very selective Boys' Grammar School when respect for authority and keenness to learn were still prevalent. Lunch hours in the 1990s were fraught with difficulties, 'invasions' from the village secondary school being commonplace. How different thirty years earlier, for while Fred Hudson, his Deputy, slept off his lunch in his room above the Office, Harry tramped halfway up St. Helen's Gate for a meal at home. On snowy days, and there were many in the

The young Dave Bush, working alongside some of the long-established King James's 'giants' in 1971.
Back row: M Binns, S Wroe, A Bamforth, I Jordan, A Gaukroger, K L W Ireland, P Heywood, J A Hargreaves, D W Gregson, R Walker
Middle row: [Groundsman], B Noble, K Wilson, [French teaching assistant], A Stockdale, Mrs Morris, A Thorpe, L Mallinson, Helen Hebblethwaite, Sam Ellis
Front row: F J Bareham, J Taylor, G W Chapman, F S Hudson, Harry Taylor, D Hinchliffe, D Clarkson, D A Bush, G Beach

The Jacobean Society was inaugurated in 1945 'for the promotion of literary, scientific and debating activities' and would become the School's most notable society. Here it is shown in 1966/7.
Back row: G R H Pogson, N D Beaumont, P M Modzelewski, R A Whiteley, R Smith, D M A Smith, S Horner, A B Irvine, M W Bevins, J Sampson
Middle row: D L Newsome, P E Keane, T H Smith, M V Sykes, J A Heap, R J Calder, S C Denton, B Sweeney, G R Morris, R B Lord, L J Orme
Front row: A R Trueman, R W Johnson, F J Bareham, L Mallinson, F S Hudson, G M Powner, Headmaster, A M Crawford, G L Beach, J P Toomey, R A Shaw, R H N Booth

responded. Advocates of comprehensive education will cite these examples as evidence to support their cause, while defenders of the old order will say they were just late developers.

Certainly there were some brilliant teachers; sadly, I have space to mention only two. In King James's 400 year history Jack Taylor must rank very highly among its most influential and colourful characters. Apart from short spells in Coventry and at Royds Hall, Jack devoted the whole of his career to teaching down St. Helen's Gate. Appointed by Harry Taylor to teach Biology, he began his dedicated service in September 1959. Although he could have retired earlier it was indicative of his devotion to his school and his profession that he retired only when forced to do so at the age of 65 in July 1997. Even then only rumours that he might have to be shot in harness ensured his departure.

Pupils and colleagues remember and recall with affection his booming voice, his outstanding exploits on the cricket and football fields, his attention to the finest detail in the setting out of written work and above all his humorous antics. It has been said that a whole book could be written containing anecdotes about Jack Taylor. One of his favourites was to detach the tubing from the fire extinguisher in his Biology Lab. and to speak down it. He claimed that this was a direct line to the Head's study. A strong man both physically and mentally, his fortitude

Jack Taylor taught at King James's from 1959 to 1997. He has retained close links with the School since his retirement and is a former chairman of the Old Almondburians' Society

1960s – even the weather appears to have changed since then – he would return and cane a few miscreants deemed to have been snowballing too close to the school buildings.

The 'Golden Years'?

These years are often regarded as King James's 'Golden Age' and in some ways they were. The school was very popular, sports teams achieved great success both at local and county level, out-of-school activities thrived and a steady stream of pupils was admitted to Oxbridge. Yet criticism was made that the school concentrated too much on its brightest students to the neglect of the weaker. The 'weaker' were, as the adjective suggests, only comparatively so. The intake was highly selective, the school admitting at one period perhaps only the top 20% of the ability range. Today all would be capable of obtaining top degrees but then those at the bottom of classes were regarded most unfairly as academically misplaced. One whom I chided on his very poor achievement appeared recently in *Who's Who of the World's Top 2000 Scientists*.

The ultimate sanction was to be 'kept down a year'. One Almondbury boy who suffered this indignity is now an eminent professor in a science department in the University of Western Australia. My colleague Jack Taylor met another at an OAS Dinner. Jack asked him where he was working. 'The University of Huddersfield,' he replied. 'And what are you studying?' queried Jack. 'I'm not a student, I lecture there,' he did fail him on one occasion. The school secretary, Doreen Hinchliffe, telephoned him to say that the Head, Alan Conley, was on his way up to the Lab and would Jack inform him that his zip was undone. Five minutes later Jack rang her back to say that his courage had deserted him. Despite this lapse it was fitting that he rose to become Senior Teacher.

It is typical of the man that he brought the same loyalty and service to the Old Almondburians' Society that he had shown as a teacher at King James's. As a past Chairman he still rarely misses an executive meeting of the Society. In addition he is a governor at the School, a great supporter of the Old Almondburians' Cricket Club – he was still turning out for them in his early 70's, and refereeing soccer matches – and a very much in demand and accomplished after dinner speaker.

To parody Mary Tudor (and perhaps appropriate for a biology teacher) Jack Taylor might justly say, 'When I am dead and opened, you will find King James's lying in my heart.'

I must also mention Patrick O'Brien. It seems highly likely that before retirement Patrick will establish an enviable record in that he could become the longest serving teacher in the history of King James's. Apart from a post graduate year in Canada, Patrick has spent his entire teaching life at King James's. He first came to the School in November 1971 on teaching practice from the University of Leeds. Ten years before, I had done exactly the same and from then on Patrick's career followed mine in a remarkably similar manner. Appointed by Harry Taylor he took up a full time post in September 1972. Junior Latin teacher became Head of Classics, Examinations Officer and time-tabler, all of which roles I had at one stage filled. In 1997 he became part of the Senior Management Team

A lifelong steam railways enthusiast, Patrick O'Brien came to King James's in 1971. Deputy Head since 2004, he could become the longest serving teacher in the history of the School

and in January 2004 assumed the position of Deputy Head.

As a great railway enthusiast, his passion was indulged by establishing a Railway Club whose layout was in the cellar under the school secretary's office. He helped to run the school scout troop and when reorganisation necessitated its closure he transferred his allegiance to the 37th in Almondbury. Some thirty years later he is still

A dedicated Almondburian, he has hardly ever missed an OAS dinner

there, an excellent example of his dedication to young people. His passion for football and for Bristol Rovers in particular – his home city – is not widely known. However, he has always been a spectator rather than a player. He did turn out for the Staff XI on two occasions. It is recorded that on the first he touched the ball twice (or more correctly it hit him) while on the second there was no actual contact whatsoever between the two.

Patrick's enthusiasm for his subject has helped to maintain the popularity and examination success of Latin and Classical Studies. He has organized frequent visits to the Classical World. His industry and efficiency in organization is legendary while his fervent desire to see King James's move to the top of the Kirklees examinations league table seems certain to be realised in the near future. A dedicated Almondburian he has hardly ever missed an OAS dinner or failed to appear with other Old Almondburians in Almondbury Church on the Sunday morning of the Dinner weekend.

But it is only fair to record that there were other teachers at best inefficient and at worst incompetent. One who was constantly late for his lessons or forgot to go; another who admitted he did not fully know the requirements of the O-level syllabus; one whose discipline was so poor that one observer said he was uncertain whether the teacher was chasing the pupils round the room or vice versa; another whose notes regarding pupils' misdemeanours were so numerous that Harry Taylor declared that, had he kept them all, they would have reached from floor to ceiling in his study; and finally the long standing member who had to leave during each lesson to worship the goddess Nicotina and allegedly place a bet with the caretaker in the boiler room. That's five and there were only 21 members of staff at the time.

The end of the Grammar School

Nevertheless the Grammar School had thrived but its days were numbered. How appropriate then that its two leaders should retire within eight months of each other. Fred Hudson FRGS (pupils suggested this stood for 'Fred runs the Grammar School') left in December 1972 while Harry Taylor retired in July of the next year. I had been appointed Acting Deputy in January 1973 so had the daunting task of organising Harry's last day. His wife, Jessica, was spirited away from Huddersfield High School to join him in his study. In almost total silence the whole school was lined up on either side of the corridors leading from the study to the assembly hall. A tap on the study door, 'We are ready, Mr Taylor,' and Harry emerged to enormous applause which accompanied him all the way to the hall. For such a cricket devotee this 'being applauded all the way to the wicket' seemed highly appropriate. A moving and memorable speech followed – Harry Taylor's eloquence was renowned (although at the opening of the 1963 extensions he did declare that some would be able to watch the Countess of Dartmouth on 'short circuit television') – perhaps a final 'humph' and a chapter closed.

After my being Acting Head for the Autumn Term Alan Conley took up his position of Head in January 1974, a post he held until

King James's Grammar School became King James's College and accepted the first girls into the sixth form in 1974. Alan Conley and Dave Bush, on the extreme right, welcome (left to right): June Bayling, Linda Taylor, Danielle Galvin, Mandy Brawn, Linda Hepplestone, Maria Lijke

footballer and athlete in his younger days and took a keen interest in King James's sporting achievements. Sadly, soon after his appointment, his wife was diagnosed with a terminal illness. His deeply held Christian beliefs sustained him during this protracted time while more turbulence created by further reorganisation in Huddersfield's education system added to his burden.

As was mentioned earlier, September 1974 saw the advent of the Sixth Form College and girls entering the school for the first time. *The Huddersfield Examiner* duly pictured this historic event on its front page and many wondered how the school would adapt to having 16-18 year old girls on the premises and in particular in the classrooms. Apart from the necessary alterations to toilet and changing facilities the changeover went very smoothly, helped by the fact that most of the Old Brigade had left or retired. However, I recall one occasion when Alan Conley had to 'have a word' with one young male colleague who had been seen at lunchtime disappearing across the playing fields with the most attractive girl of the year.

But the College barely survived its infancy. September 1976 saw the first 13-18 comprehensive intake and insufficient buildings on the site to accommodate them. The solution to this problem and other changes in the environment are covered later. Alan retired in July 1985. He moved to the South West where he could devote more time to his ministry, spend time with his new wife and take a pass-

HEADMASTER FACTFILE 1608-2008

NAME Alan Conley
DATE OF APPOINTMENT 1974
DATE OF DEPARTURE 1985
DEGREE BSc
UNIVERSITY Durham
LIFE IN BRIEF

Alan Conley's appointment saw him take charge of what was in effect two schools on one site; the new Sixth Form College and the last years of the Boys' Grammar School. The decision to abort the former meant the advent of the first 13-18 mixed comprehensive intake in 1976 and the two schools becoming for a short time three on a split site.

To his great credit he managed to maintain staff morale during these difficult days and when he retired in 1985 to Thornford near Sherborne in Dorset to become the Rev J A Conley he left a thriving and popular comprehensive school.

23

July 1985. A Mancunian and ardent Manchester City fan, Alan had been an outstanding

ing interest in Yeovil Town. He is remembered as a great supporter of the OAS and with affection by his former colleagues and pupils. The latter still regularly swap 'Conleyisms', a variation on Spoonerisms. 'A vicious triangle', 'keeping one's ear

HEADMASTER
FACTFILE
1608-2008

NAME	Clive Watkins
DATE OF APPOINTMENT	1985
DATE OF DEPARTURE	1998
DEGREE	LLB
UNIVERSITY	Liverpool
LIFE IN BRIEF	Although a Liverpudlian by birth, Clive Watkins arrived at King James's from Penistone where he had been Deputy Head. His legal training and outstanding command of both spoken and written English stood him in good stead when faced with the considerable difficulties presented by union militancy, Ofsted inspections, increased power of governors and budget constraints.

24

The loss of the sixth form and many experienced staff in 1990 was seen by many as a morale-sapping blow but to his great credit Clive Watkins set about creating a popular 11-16 Comprehensive. His devotion to building further success most probably accounts for his needing major heart surgery and consequent premature retirement.

to the grindstone' are two fine examples. As corporal punishment was still permitted and he was reluctant for it to be administered to girls he faced a dilemma. He was not sure where we stood 'since this Sexual Relations Act'.

His successor faced no such verbal challenges. Clive Watkins, a Liverpudlian, who took up the King James's reins in September 1985, soon proved himself a master of both the spoken and written word. A lawyer by training, Clive had devoted himself to the teaching of English yet somehow found time to write prize-winning poetry. Indeed, in his retirement his poetic exploits have led to wide travel and international acclaim. I wrote 'somehow found time' for Clive was one of hardest working colleagues I have ever known. Additionally Clive had to face pressures which would have been inconceivable in the 1960s. The increased power of the school governors, the militancy of the trade unions, the advent of league tables and Ofsted inspections, more stringent health and safety regulations and the change to an 11-16 school with the consequent loss of very experienced staff to Greenhead College placed an intolerable burden on him. It was no surprise when he suffered a serious heart attack in December 1997. This resulted in his having a heart-bypass operation and eventually being allowed to take early retirement. As stalwarts Senior

Teacher, Jack Taylor and Deputy Head, Pat Reid, had retired in July 1997 in just under four terms the school had lost its whole Senior Management Team.

Another four terms were to pass with various people holding various acting positions including Dr. Sheila Kaye as Head before Martin Shevill arrived from Honley High in April 1999 to take up the permanent post. For a King James's Head Martin's tenure was comparatively short for he moved on to Ossett at the end of 2002. On January 1st 2003 Robert Lamb arrived from t'other side of t'Pennines to assume the Headship. A summary of their stewardship is covered elsewhere but it is interesting to note that King James's has had only five heads in the last 56 years and that the Lancastrians outnumber the Yorkshiremen by three to two.

So how does the school which Robert inherited in 2003 differ physically from the one I entered in 1961? In a word, enormously, both in terms of the actual buildings and the grounds that surround them. Inevitably too, for, as mentioned earlier, the school now caters for more than twice as many pupils as it did in the 1960s. The 1963 additions had seen a new assembly hall/gymnasium, music practice rooms and a dining room. The latter had meant the end of the 'Woodnut' (Wooden Hut) being used for school dinners where Frank Anderson used to order the windows to be flung open on the coldest of days to 'let some air into this steaming hole'. Its partial use as a

HEADMASTER
FACTFILE
1608-2008

NAME	Martin Shevill
DATE OF APPOINTMENT	1999
DATE OF DEPARTURE	2002
DEGREE	B Ed, M Sc
UNIVERSITIES	Leeds, Sheffield Hallam
LIFE IN BRIEF	Martin Shevill arrived at King James's after a spell at nearby Honley High School as Deputy Head, having previously working as a teacher in Sheffield and briefly as a university lecturer at Sheffield University. He is a geographer and was the author of a number of school textbooks before moving into senior management positions.

25

During Martin Shevill's relatively brief stewardship of the school an extensive building programme took place that involved extensions to the science and music areas along with imaginative internal remodelling to create a gymnasium, drama studio and library. The Student Council was also established in his time. It was also the period when government legislation began to increase significantly the accountability of schools.

Language Laboratory saw Helen Hebblethwaite become the first lady to join the staff since the war years. It was often said that pupils would deliberately sabotage their machines so that the ample Mrs H. would lean over them to effect repairs. After numerous changes of use the Woodnut is now the Year 11 Common Room but is 'wood' no more; it is now faced with the same attractive stone as the surrounding buildings. The small room at the end, the staff dining room when I first came to King James's, later the Scouts' storeroom, is now the caretakers' abode. Clearly it is impossible to enumerate all the changes, fascinating as they are, so a selection must be made. However, description is not easy since room names have been changed to strictly numerical terms, a most regrettable move in my opinion and one which leads to confusion among former pupils. I shall adhere to the old nomenclature. Of the 'D's only D1 remains as a teaching room, the 'N's have rooms built into the loft space above and The Big (library), for a short time abandoned as such in the 1980s to become a classroom, has reverted, thankfully, to its original use.

I think lots were drawn for the one who was to inform me that 'Big Tree' had been felled

The change to comprehensive

The most fundamental changes since 1608 were necessitated by the change to comprehensive status in September 1976. Substantial new buildings were required but were only at the planning stage. As the Kayes – 'He and I dyd shifte it' – had moved the school down St. Helen's Gate in 1547 so 429 years later a good portion was shifted back to the top of the hill, in fact into Fenay Lane. Actually, a similar situation had arisen fifty-seven years earlier although on a much smaller scale. Expansion had necessitated the use of the Wesleyan schoolroom in the village from 1919 to 1923.

The Fenay Lane site had been occupied by various schools in the past and was also the location of the caretaker's large house. Today it is covered by a modern housing estate. Pupils of this era will have vivid memo-

ries of regular trudges up and down St. Helen's while teachers improved their physical fitness or used their cars – some even claimed mileage allowance – as they alternated their teaching venue. For me as timetabler, a nightmare. I do not recall a single accident as pupils left the narrow driveway, crossed the busy road and descended St. Helen's. I do remember, however, Dave Gregson, a most religious man, clipping the wall on entry to the schoolyard, cracking the perspex on his rear cluster lights and being appalled at the cost. On tightening up the replacement, he screwed it up too tightly and cracked it once more. His reaction was, to say the least, memorable. A new two storey, seven classroom teaching block, a splendid craft area and large sports hall meant that all teaching eventually was back on one site.

The temporary classrooms on the lawn in front of the library disappeared. It was here that once a dumper truck partially demolished the corner of one while Alan Conley was conducting a Maths lesson therein. Outside enormous earth movers had carved out a level surface for an all-weather athletics track and hockey pitch where the third, ever-muddy soccer field had been and where a junior Art teacher had once refereed a match in wellingtons and gown. The slope running up towards Grasscroft was gouged out to provide tennis courts and an additional pitch. The old tennis courts at the bottom of the Bunk became a bus bay. Even Big Tree was eventually to fall. So symbolic, it had dominated the playground for generations. Declared unsafe by the bursar at the time, the Old Almondburians' Society paid for a professional survey. An arborist reported that with judicial pruning Big Tree would stand for many more years. It seemed to have been saved but staff and pupils returning to school after the Easter holidays in 1997 were shocked to see it had been felled. I think lots were drawn for the one who was to inform me. In Spring 2004 King James's School was granted Specialist Science College Status. The fact that a splendid new Science building now covers Big Tree's site does soften the blow a little.

The older generation will regret that on the Sunday afternoon of Founders' Day Weekend in late November pupils and parents no longer gather under Big Tree's almost leafless canopy for the annual ascent of St. Helen's and the service in Almondbury Parish Church. Changes in attitude exacerbated by transport difficulties meant the demise of this moving event in the School's calendar. However, other traditions live on. It may now be called 'Presentation Evening' rather than 'Speech Day' but this impressive occasion still takes place every year in Huddersfield Town Hall. Prominent Old Almondburians such as Ryan Sidebottom (Yorkshire, Nottinghamshire and England cricketer), Derek Ibbotson (World Mile record holder) and Gorden Kaye (TV star of *'Allo, 'Allo*) have been among those presenting the prizes.

The House System is preserved. It is always gratifying and surprising at OAS dinners to hear the passions aroused when a certain House is mentioned. When a set of four younger house masters was appointed by Harry Taylor in the mid sixties, rivalry became fierce. Fenay's dominance was at last broken. There was no Walter Haigh who, it is claimed, regularly gathered up all the spikes in the PE Department and on Sports Day distrib-

uted them among the Fenay runners. Dartmouth, Fenay and Siddon now took turns in becoming Cock House; but not Jessop! As Jessop Housemaster I had even resorted to breeding my own (my son Alan attended the School from 1972-79, naturally as a member of Jessop). Jessop had been Champion House in the late forties. How ironic that the year after I left Jessop seized the coveted title in 1997. Shortly afterwards two new houses were added, Bush and Taylor, 'in recognition of the long service of these two teachers'. Yet this system simply did not work and though I had felt most honoured, the traditionalist in me was quietly pleased by the reversion to the original four, introduced by Taylor Dyson in 1915. Bush v Jessop no longer divides my loyalties.

Health and Safety regulations, the majority of pupils being bussed in and promptly out at the end of the school day, the proliferation of after-school staff meetings, increased demands in the classroom ... all these have led to a great diminution in voluntary club and society activities. The 1960s and 1970s had produced an impressive list. Scientific, Philatelic, Railway, Printing, Classics, Chess, Orchestra, Photographic are examples. Even a Honey Bear Appreciation Society (cereal packet) was discovered holding a meeting, minutes being taken, in the Old Book Room although it was suspected that this was to avoid having to go outside on a wintry day.

I have deliberately omitted two from the original list for they considered themselves to be doyens: the Jacobean Debating Society and the Scout Troop. Many Old Almondburians have expressed profound indebtedness to these institutions for the confidence, sense of duty and enjoyment which they derived from membership. A photograph, dated 1971, reveals that 25% of staff and 17% of pupils were involved in scouting. Sporting activities also flourished. If selected to play for the school at football on a Saturday morning or cricket on a summer's Saturday afternoon the player was expected to attend and in full school uniform. Staff also took their turn either by refereeing or umpiring at home or accompanying the team away. Most time-consuming and consequently it is hardly surprising that such commitments are now restricted to Wednesday afternoons. To conclude on a positive note, it should be mentioned that one area that has seen a significant increase, a reflection perhaps of

The arrival of girls during Dave Bush's time at King James's was welcomed by boys who hitherto had to take girls' parts. This is the cast of the 1986 production of 'My Fair Lady'

The last sixth form at King James's School, photographed on a sunny day in 1989 in front of the Library. In 1990, the School took on its present role as a co-educational comprehensive for the age group 11 - 16

society at large, is the frequency of groups travelling abroad not infrequently to quite exotic locations.

The teachers leading these parties are, of course, all graduates. Teaching has been an all-graduate profession for many years now. This was not the case when I arrived at King James's. On Founders' Day, as the staff assembled at the head of the procession about to wend its way up St. Helen's Gate, I always felt sorry and almost embarrassed for the non-graduates dressed only in their Sunday best while the graduates were resplendent in their gowns, hoods and mortar boards. No ladies initially but Mrs Hebblethwaite, mentioned earlier, was followed in 1972 by Marie Oosterwyk whose arrival created quite a stir in the staffroom. In the case of English teacher Alan Thomas particularly so, for he married her later the same year. This surely must have been the first marriage between members of the King James's teaching staff although Fred Bungeroth had married the school secretary in the 1950s. The number of females gradually increased and rapidly accelerated when the school became mixed from 1974 onwards. Whenever a new female appointment was made Ken Ireland, PE teacher, would declare 'not another b****y woman. She won't be taking the under-13s.' It was rumoured that Ken had never properly recovered from the 'Fun Day' when the younger ladies on the staff had turned up *à la St. Trinian's* in full school uniform. Ken had to leave the staffroom. Today of the full time staff 35% are male and 65 % are female, a pattern that is repeated in most state secondary schools.

It has already been mentioned that the advent of girls into the school did not appear to create too many problems for the teachers. I feel a much greater one was posed by the wide range in academic ability of the new

intake. Almost overnight – in effect over the summer holidays – with no additional training staff who had previously taught only in the Grammar School or the Sixth Form College had to adapt to most unfamiliar situations.

Again, my personal experiences illustrate what most colleagues must have endured. I found myself moving from a small A-level Latin class where we had been working our way through Tacitus's *Agricola* to face 25 bottom-set Classical Studies students. In their previous lesson I had described in simple terms Virgil's description of Aeneas's *Flight from Troy* and had asked them to re-tell the story for that night's homework. How was I to explain to one girl that she had not quite grasped the point when she had Aeneas packing his case and catching a flight at Heathrow? And how to respond to the Year 11 girl who well into her course asked, 'Mr Bush, didn't the ancient Greeks make their sandals out of old car tyres?' Failure to understand was, of course, as much my problem as theirs and a very salutary lesson for me. It certainly kept us all on our pedagogical toes. Not surprisingly the loss of the Sixth Form in 1990 caused a major exodus of staff. Teaching at A-level was always the icing on the classroom cake. The attractions of almost exclusively A-level work at the rapidly expanding, most successful and nationally recognised Greenhead Sixth Form

... the loss of the Sixth Form in 1990 caused a major exodus of staff

College proved irresistible for them but they did show their interest in and affection for the school by joining the OAS. It is said that the only pressure these teachers face at Greenhead is centred on the drive to produce outstanding examination results. They may dispute this but King James's staff will say they too have this. In addition, the constant demand, as in all state secondary schools, to maintain order and discipline is most wearing. Was school life so much simpler in the 1960s?

Certainly examination results did not arouse such intense interest and rivalry as today's League Tables. An early staff meeting was memorable for me in that the GCSE results were glossed over in under five minutes while a discussion as to whether cutlery should be given out before or after grace roused heated arguments. Parents then rarely had immediate access to a phone; consequently contact with school was rare. The advent of the mobile phone now means that as the first snowflake falls the school office phone rings constantly with enquiries as to whether the pupils are being sent home early.

Some of the major misdemeanors that merited the cane in the Headmaster's study in the late 1950s. Harry Taylor kept meticulous notes in his 'Punishment Book', even recording the number of strokes of the cane received by each unfortunate miscreant

This simple example illustrates how schools are so much more accessible, more accountable, so much more society-centred than they were 50 years ago. After almost silently climbing Somerset Road the trolley buses at that time discharged their young passengers at the Almondbury terminus from where they descended St Helen's Gate to pass another almost cloistered day. Society has changed enormously since then and schools are but a microcosm of society at large. It would be naïve to suggest that parental separation and divorce, the availability of drugs, alcohol and sexual activity did not exist in the sixties but certainly not on the scale of today. Peer pressure is often an irresistible force. Yet it is doubtful if intrinsically pupils have changed much over 50 years.

Outwardly they have. The 11 year old who entered through Big Tree Yard in September 2007 would smile if not guffaw should his friend stand alongside him dressed in the uniform of 1961. The only common denominator would be the black and yellow striped tie. His early counterpart would be resplendent in school blazer, short trousers, grey socks, grey pullover and school cap

It is doubtful if pupils have changed much over 50 years

with his house colours displayed on a band at the back. Back in 1961 at the end of his first day the chances were that his sartorial elegance would have been somewhat diminished after the initiation ceremony of being pushed down the Bunk into the holly bushes. One can imagine the reactions of modern parents to that. The demise of the blazer was regretted by some, for its capacious pockets could hold so many treasures. Today dark trousers or skirt, school tie and pullover emblazoned with school crest suffice.

Corporal punishment

My belief that pupils have undergone little intrinsic change is supported by a recent discovery made during an attempt to sort through archive material in the storeroom above the Head's study: the Punishment Book. By law a record had to be kept of all corporal punishment administered by the head or his delegated authority. Some forty pages cover the period from Harry Taylor's appointment in September 1951 to Alan Conley's last entry on 24th November 1984 when presumably corporal punishment was abolished. I am sure P. Boothroyd of Form 4 never realised he was making school history when he felt the swish of the cane on that day for 'failing to turn up for detention'.

These pages are worthy of publication in full. They are so revealing and if one ignores the pain involved frequently hilarious. May a few examples suffice. 'Four boys. Stealing plums from school garden' and one whose name was added as he thought it 'unfair his name had been omitted from the original list'. '4B 2 strokes – noise outside Music Room'. The whole form? HT's arm must have ached! 'Arson'; 'Bogus telephone calls';

'Lighting incense in master's desk before he entered room'; 'Amorous interchanges at the baths during school swimming gala'; 'Jumping from window of D1 into Fenay Quad'.

However, these are amusing exceptions. What supports my belief is the frequency over thirty years with which certain offences recur. 'Smoking, truancy, forgery of notes, gambling both on horses and cards, cheek to and swearing at teachers, cutting lessons and detentions, bullying' all lead one to conclude that little has changed over those years. Perhaps recent heads can confirm this is still the case? It would be so reassuring to believe that, despite their being outwardly so worldly wise, today's King James's students are not that different from their predecessors.

Before concluding this article, one body ever closely involved with the school deserves a special mention. I refer to the Old Almondburians' Society, founded in its present format in 1920 and claimed to be one of the largest if not *the* largest organisation of its kind of any state school in the country. The first meetings I attended were in the dreadfully smoke-laden private room at the Albert. Different locations followed. I was delighted to hear recently that the OAS now meets in the Woolpack, always considered as the school's local. To become the Society's chairman was once a coveted honour; nowadays it is at times difficult to find anyone willing to take on that role. This is a reflection of people's multifarious commitments rather than lack of interest in their *alma mater*. However, the fact that its aims and objectives have not changed with the passage of time, its sheer size, the annual dinner, two excellent magazines each year and a comprehensive new website all prove its vitality. In addition, it has raised many thousands of pounds for the school and continues to do so. This is a very special organisation supporting a very special school.

I am sure descendants of Gerald Hinchliffe's rabbits still frisk on the lawn in front of the Old Schoolhouse. The view from the cricket field down the Farnley Valley remains breath-taking. The turned stone tiles on the library roof are so beautiful especially in the rain. The autumn tints on the trees on the far side of Farnley Line lift the spirits. These delights have not changed in any way. How fortunate all have been to teach and learn in such an environment! The school today is vastly oversubscribed, its examination results among the best in Kirklees. There is just cause for celebration and optimism. Yet as we celebrate 400 years of education on this site we would be well advised to bear in mind the words of that great headmaster, Taylor Dyson, when in 1944 he referred to King James's as being 'the only genuine historic school in the town' and again in 1945 when he pleaded that those who followed 'should see to it that the old school is just slightly different from any other school; that it should keep its soul whoever possesses its body.' How much our beloved School has changed in its 400 year history and more so in the last 50 than ever before. It remains incumbent upon us and on 'those who follow' to ensure that many future generations enjoy what thousands of Almondburians have enjoyed already. ◼

THE WIT AND WISDOM OF KING JAMES'S

MY UNCLE BILL

My Uncle Bill, who's ninety-eight
Is always very obstinate.
He likes to fancy he's in pain,
And, Tuesday, when it came again,
I said I'd get the doctor down.
The doctor came and, with a frown,
'What's wrong?' he asked, and Uncle Bill
Replied to him, 'I'm feeling ill.'
The doctor tried a test or two
Then said, 'There's nothing wrong with you.'
'I say there is!' old uncle cried.
'I say there's not!' the doc replied.
They went on arguing all the day
But Bill would have it his own way,
And just to prove that he was right
He died at twelve o'clock that night.

J Finlayson (IIIb, 1933)

Putting the endowments on a more secure Foundation

The School receives thousands of pounds each year from the King James's School Foundation. GRAHAM CLIFFE recalls the major campaign to secure these assets

IN THE SUMMER OF 1975 a number of Old Almondburians with an interest in cricket became aware that, because of the game's decline in schools generally, the beautiful ground in Arkenley Lane was no longer being used on Saturday afternoons. And so the idea of forming an Old Almondburians' Cricket Club and entering a team in one of the local leagues was born.

I was at the time a member of the Huddersfield YMCA Cricket Club but I was immediately attracted by the prospect of returning to the ground where I had learnt the game in the early 1960s.

I thus became a founder member of the Club which played out its first season in the glorious summer of 1976. The headmaster of the School at that time was Alan Conley and he had given the venture his full support asking only that we pay a nominal rent and that we 'take care of the pavilion'. This we were more than happy to do but I did not know at that time (nor, it seems, did anyone else closely connected with the School) that the cricket field was in fact owned by the King James's School Foundation, a trust fund dating from the seventeenth century. The affairs of the fund itself were shrouded in mystery and probably for understandable reasons in the light of subsequent events.

For my own part, I could not at that time have anticipated that my close involvement with the Old Almondburians' Cricket Club and the Old Almondburians' Society over the next thirty

years would eventually involve me and others in a long and detailed investigation into the administration of that trust fund and ultimately the recovery of hundreds of thousands of pounds of which it had been deprived.

A brief history of the Trust Fund

From the time of the school charter in 1608, a piece of land was enclosed and conveyed to the Foundation to be held for the purposes of the School and occupied by the School in perpetuity. This represents an area of approximately 2.8 acres and that covers what might now be described as the oldest part of the School.

The assets of the foundation grew over the years with gifts from various benefactors. Particularly noteworthy was the winding-up of Wormall's Charity in about 1880 and the subsequent transfer of its assets to the King James's trust. This is no doubt how the fund now comes to be the owner of the building which we all know as Almondbury Conservative Club but which was originally Wormall Hall erected in 1631.

In 1922, when the School came under the formal control of the old Huddersfield Corporation, the council became the trustee of the fund and in 1974, on local government reorganisation, that responsibility passed to the new Kirklees Metropolitan Council. In 1987, largely because the fund had been dormant for many years, a new scheme was approved by the Charity Commission with Kirklees Metro-

Graham Cliffe attended King James's from 1959 - 66. He studied Law at the University of Manchester and initially trained as a solicitor. In 1988 he became County Court Registrar, a function which in due course became designated District Judge, and in 2000 he was appointed a Circuit Judge. Today, he is a designated Family Judge for York and North Yorkshire, specialising in family law issues but also undertaking some civil cases. He played a leading role in the legal action which led to the setting up of the King James's School Foundation. Graham is a former chairman of the Old Almondburians' Society who has the distinction of living within a stone's (or possibly a cricket ball's) throw of the School cricket field at the top of Arkenley Lane.

politan Council as the sole corporate trustee, but it seems in hindsight that that was done without any proper consideration by the Charity Commission of the fund's recent financial history. All was not well with the affairs of the King James's School Foundation!

None of the history of the fund was known to Alan Conley in 1975. I understand that he became aware of the existence of the fund only shortly before he retired from the school in 1985. Obviously that was a strange state of affairs given that Kirklees Council was supposed to be administering the fund for the benefit of the School.

The Old Almondburians' Cricket Club continued to flourish throughout the 1980s and into the 1990s, rising through the various divisions and winning a number of championships and cup competitions. The club remained faithful to its promise to Alan Conley, maintaining the pavilion and completely replacing the pavilion roof on one occasion. Boys from the School were constantly encouraged to play for the club and several of them did so over a number of years with great distinction.

However, in 1994 the school and Kirklees Council gave notice that they wanted to change the arrangements under which the cricket club occupied the field. It was suggested at that time that the playing of cricket in School was very limited and that the School had no further use for the pavilion. It was also said that boys at the School could learn to play cricket indoors (obviously a comment from someone who had never played the game!).

A Council official even went so far as to suggest that the pavilion could be demolished and this came as a con-

siderable shock to members of the Society and the cricket club. It had never previously been suggested by the School that they were prepared to relinquish the facility. No credit, it seems, was to be given to the Old Almondburians' Cricket Club for the work that it had done on the pavilion over a number of years – indeed suggestions were made that the club had effectively had a free ride. This created tension between the club and the School which was hardly surprising given the part that the pavilion has in the recent history of the School. It was opened in 1958 and was partly funded by contributions from the Old Almondburians' Society. Thereafter it played an important part in the sporting life of the school. The suggestion that it was now surplus to requirements and could be demolished was met firstly by a sense of dismay and then a degree of anger on the part of the members of the cricket club who were not prepared to submit to short-sighted policies by the School and the council with no regard for the sporting welfare of future generations or the traditions of the School in which the playing of cricket had been important.

As soon as the cricket club contended that it had

All was not well with the affairs of the King James's School Foundation ...

acquired an annual tenancy of the ground (something which was arguable but by no means certain as a result of the loose arrangement arrived at with Alan Conley) matters began to be dealt with on a much more formal basis. Ownership of the cricket field by the trust fund was confirmed and it seemed to me reasonable to start making some enquiries about the administration of this fund. The accounts of a properly administered charitable trust are available for any member of the public to see and inspect. Immediately, it became apparent that Kirklees Council had not filed any accounts for a period of seven years.

The official at the Charity Commission who disclosed this was obviously embarrassed. The Commission was supposed to have systems in place which would prevent this situation arising but, for whatever reason, they had failed and the council was therefore told to put matters in order. A number of deadlines were given to the council for the filing of accounts but they were ignored. At times the process, which took about two years, proved to be tiresome but as far as the cricketers were concerned the stakes were high. Essentially the question was whether the field and the pavilion were to be lost forever. I continued to put pressure on the Charity Commission and ultimately Kirklees Council filed accounts but it was obvious that those accounts had been reconstructed in reverse order. The accounts raised far more questions than they answered.

Even at this juncture, the Charity Commission seemed to be reluctant to take vigorous action and the council's policy was obviously one of continued delay and obfuscation. By chance, in 1997, I attended a dinner at the Law Society in London and found myself seated next to a former Charity Commissioner. I took the opportunity of explaining the problem to him and he put me in touch with a named individual at the Charity Commission office in Liverpool. Things then began to move more quickly.

We were fortunate at that stage in being able to call upon the help of Nigel Priestley, an Old Almondburian and a practising Solicitor. He devoted many hours of his time in correspondence with the Charity Commission and together with myself and Richard Taylor (eldest son of Harry Taylor and a playing member of the Old Almondburians' Cricket Club) he attended a meeting at the Charity Commission in June of 1998. We were able to emphasise our concerns about the administration of the trust and the growing feeling that it had been deprived of funds for very many years.

As more information began to trickle out, it was realised that the cricket field was but a small part of the assets of the fund. We discovered that the fund owned houses in Westgate (as well as the Almondbury Conservative Club). There were also the freehold inter-

ests in properties in Wormald Street in Almondbury and in Swallow Lane in Golcar. In addition, the fund held bonds and investments and pieces of land in Arkenley Lane and Sharp Lane in Almondbury. The Charity Commission was persuaded to launch a formal inquiry and although the council continued with its efforts to frustrate a proper investigation, a report was issued in March of 1999. It was critical of the council in a number of respects and it was perhaps best summed up by the investigating officer when he said:

The council are completely neglecting their duties as trustee, and this failure to involve themselves is one of the most significant areas of concern to me.

The writing was on the wall and Kirklees Council was clearly going to lose control of the trust fund one way or another. They nevertheless then began a furious rearguard action to try to punish the cricket club and to

Solicitor and Old Almondburian Nigel Priestley played a leading role in the discussions to unravel the intricacies of the School's ancient endowments

The out-of-court settlement attracted considerable publicity in the press. This story appeared within days in The Huddersfield Daily Examiner

avoid any member of the Old Almondburians' Society becoming one of the trustees under a newly constituted scheme. In 1998, the council locked the gates to the cricket field and denied the cricket club access. It planted a large number of saplings on the car park area. It was infantile behaviour on the part of council officials and when Nigel Priestley took them to court they were ordered to allow the cricket club immediate access and they were also ordered to dig up and remove all of the saplings and pay the cricket club's legal costs. It seems that, at that time, their high handed behaviour knew no bounds but they were clearly not aware of either the determination or the combined talents of the members of the Old Almondburians' Society.

The council turned its attention to the individual members of the Old Almondburians' Society who had been proposed as potential new trustees. Their intemperate comments about the qualities of some of those individuals led to threats of further legal action but ultimately the Charity Commission became so tired of the council's delaying tactics that it imposed a new scheme in September of 2001 since which time the fund has been administered by eight individual trustees. I became the chairman of trustees at that time and continue in that capacity.

The New Scheme

Once the new trustees were in place, it became easier to obtain documentation about the past administration of the fund. It quickly became clear that the fund had been neglected from 1951 onwards and very probably from as far back as 1922.

The trustees began to contemplate the exercise of trying to determine what this fund ought to have been worth had Huddersfield Corporation and Kirklees Council done the job that they were delegated to do. The task was daunting, but again the Old Almondburians' Society had among its membership lawyers, surveyors and accountants (including a forensic accountant) who were all prepared to give the benefit of their expertise. Nigel Priestley continued to work tirelessly to bring matters to a successful conclusion.

Officials of the council were invited to discuss the issues with a view to reaching an amicable settlement. They simply refused and alleged that there was no loss to the trust fund. They apparently lapsed into an extended period of sulking and the trustees were therefore left with no alternative but to issue proceedings in the Chancery Division of the High Court in Manchester. The council was brought to heel, no doubt influenced by the looming prospect of individual officers and councillors giving evidence in an attempt to defend the indefensible. They finally agreed to mediate and on the 27th April 2004, a meeting was arranged at the George Hotel in Huddersfield attended by three trustees including myself and also a solicitor acting on behalf of the trust. The council was represented by a number of officials from its legal, finance and education departments and their team was led by a barrister from London. The mediation was chaired by an experienced legal mediator from London but there was a further presence at the meeting which ultimately, in my view, proved to be decisive.

In any proceedings involving charitable trusts HM Attorney General has to be included as a defendant. This

In the last financial year the trustees were able to make grants to the School totalling more than £60,000

is because the Attorney General is considered to be the guardian of charitable trusts and his role is to ensure that no settlement is reached which is detrimental to the interests of the beneficiaries i.e. the young people attending King James's School. To the surprise of many of us, and to the obvious dismay of Kirklees Council, the Attorney General decided to be represented at the mediation by the Treasury Solicitor. He set out his position in a document which he lodged with all parties seven days before the meeting at the George Hotel. The Attorney General did not so much fire a warning shot across their bows but chose instead to torpedo them well below the water line. Through his representative he said:

> 'When a local authority acts as trustee of a charitable trust its duties as trustee are identical to those which would be incumbent on any other trustee. The fact that it is an elected public body is irrelevant to that proposition. If in any particular case the interest of the charity appears to be contrary to what the local authority considers to those of its tax payers, the interest of the charity must prevail.'

The mediation lasted for a total of fifteen hours but

this marathon session resulted in the fund being compensated to the tune of hundreds of thousands of pounds. The council wanted a confidentiality clause (and it was obvious why) but they then proceeded to disclose the figure and discuss it in an open council meeting!

The Present Arrangements

The trustees now meet on about five or six occasions each year to consider applications by the School for funds and also to review the performance of the investments. The trustees are all people with a keen interest in the welfare of the School. We have a clerk who deals with the day to day administration and there is no doubt that the School is very fortunate to be able to benefit from the fund. The capital value of properties owned and other investments is probably now in the region of £2 million. In the last financial year the trustees were able to make grants to the School totalling more than £60,000. Income of that order is likely to be available indefinitely. The fund that was decimated by successive local authorities was restored by the Old Almondburians' Society. The members can be proud that in this regard they have truly 'upheld the status and honour of the School.' ◗

Looking to the future with optimism and confidence

Present Head Teacher ROBERT LAMB saw many challenges when he arrived at the School in 2003. But today he leads a successful and over-subscribed King James's

BEFORE DECIDING TO APPLY for the Headship at King James's I drove over to have a look at the School. Friends who live in the Huddersfield area had told me that I must apply. They had told me all about the reputation and history of the School. The more they

told me the more intrigued and interested I became.

So I set out one Sunday afternoon in June 2002 to have a look at the School. Like many people before me and no doubt many people in the future I reached Almondbury easily but then got lost and couldn't find it. I was directed down Sharp Lane and approached the School via Arkenley Lane. As soon as I saw it my mind was made up. It looked stunning. The front of the School looked as though it was from another era and the setting was magnificent. I wondered what it must have been like in years gone by. I drove home and immediately applied for the job.

Interview day arrived and I was given the customary tour of the School. My first impression was that it looked wonderful from the outside with its listed buildings and the idyllic setting. However the interior was a different story. I must admit that it came as a bit of a shock. I had

never been in a school that had such narrow corridors and so many nooks and crannies. I was surprised at the many small and almost dilapidated rooms, the state of decoration and the lack of basic resources throughout the School.

It was obvious that the School had suffered from many years of poor and inadequate funding. Later investigation led me to discover that it was one of the worst funded schools in the whole of Kirklees. The buildings hardly seemed fit for 21st century education.

But the big plus were the people. Everyone I met was absolutely wonderful. Their warmth and friendliness were a delight. They all spoke highly of the school and clearly had an affection and love for it. Any remaining doubts disappeared when the then Deputy Head Boy took me on the playing fields and said 'Let me take you over here, Sir, and show you a view that I am particularly fond of.' I was determined to get the job and was ecstatic when I was appointed the 26th Headteacher of King James's School.

It was obvious that one of my first tasks was to generate

Education, 2008 style: Students hard at work computing in the ICT (Information and Communication Technology) room

extra money to give the students and staff the facilities and resources that they deserved. On taking up the post, in January 2003, I investigated extra funding opportunities. We managed to get extra funding to renovate a Science room and further funding to renovate some of the Design rooms. But these would not make the difference that was required. The school needed a lot spent on it. This was

Languages but the close proximity of another Language College at Almondbury High School led to a change of plan. It was rather apt however to apply for Science College status considering the part that Science had played in the history of the school. In the 1850s the initiatives of Rev Alfred Easther and George Jarmain had put the school at the forefront of scientific education. In fact in 1863 the school took six 'hard to win' Queen's prizes in Chemistry and Jarmain was described as 'the outstanding teacher of Chemistry in the North.'

The writing of the bid had already been started by the Head of Mathematics, David Bradford, and it looked promising. A small committee of Governors and friends of the school was formed to generate ideas and funding. Pippa Dodgshon (then Deputy Headteacher) and I then worked with David to ensure that the bid was strong. But the problem was not the writing of the bid but the generating of the £50,000 we needed to submit a bid. The King James's School Foundation had promised £25,000 and the Old Almondburians Society £5,000 but no other funding had been secured.

I then received a phone call from local resident Michael Woodhead. Although Michael had had no connections with King James's he wanted to do something to help his local school. He kindly offered to use his contacts to seek possible sponsors in order to generate the missing £20,000. Thanks to his efforts and generosity a further £15,000 was promised. This left us just £5,000 short. Walter Raleigh then organised a sponsored walk to Castle Hill and back. The students, their parents and friends got behind this and the missing £5,000 was raised with ease.

We submitted the bid in September 2003 and discovered in early January 2004 that we had been successful. As you can imagine we were ecstatic. This was so important for the future success of the School and it wouldn't have been possible without the support, generosity and hard work of so many people. Thanks are due to all our sponsors, but particularly to Michael Woodhead for his hard work and powers of persuasion and to Bob Williams (class of 1971 and Membership Secretary of the Old

This board on prominent display at the School lists the sponsors whose generosity led to its achievement of Specialist Science College status in 2004

made abundantly clear on practically every visit from an Old Boy who always commented that the Science rooms are just as they remembered them. Comments you could accept from someone who left in the last ten years but many of the remarks came from people who had left in the 1950s. It was therefore crucial to achieve Specialist College status in order to generate the Capital Grant of £150,000 and annual funding of £100,000.

The School had decided before my appointment to apply for specialist status in Science. There had previously been talk about applying for specialist status in

Almondburians' Society) whose experience of writing bids proved invaluable.

The capital funding of £150,000 and other grants was put towards improving our facilities and resources. In the summer of 2004, two of the out-dated Science labs were renovated and state-of-the-art Information and Communication Technology (ICT) equipment purchased. It gave the School a real lift. Since then further grants and the generosity of the King James's School Foundation has allowed us to improve the interior of the School even more. We have extended a number of our classrooms and purchased ICT equipment that makes us the envy of the vast majority of schools.

Science College status has definitely given the School a real boost. Examination results in Science and Mathematics (the subsidiary subject of Science College status) have risen year on year and are now at unprecedented levels. The general academic results of the School have also risen from 51% of students achieving 5A*-C in 2003 to 71% achieving 5A*-C now. This incredible increase in results has led to many accolades including being named, by the government, as one of the most improved schools in the country. We were one of only two schools in the whole of West Yorkshire to receive this accolade and it is something that everyone associated with the School can be justifiably proud of.

(Left to right)
Worthy winners of the new 2006/7 indoor five-a-side football league: Jordan Andrade, Matt Grist, Alex Holmes, Scott Preene, Matthew Warrington. King James's is fortunate in having one of the finest sports halls in the area

These successes have led to a massive increase in the popularity of the School. It is consistently over-subscribed and as soon as a student leaves their place is filled almost immediately. This increase in popularity led to the Governors requesting that the number of places available in each year group be increased from 160 to 180. This request was granted by Kirklees and was introduced in September 2007. Despite the increase in places we have the longest waiting list in the history of the School.

The problem now is where to put everyone. Temporary classrooms have once again been placed on the lawn in front of the library to give us extra classroom space but the corridors, dining facilities and layout of the School still causes us many problems. The School will be rebuilt sometime in the future under the government's *Building Schools for the Future* scheme but the earliest date is likely to be 2015. But where will the School be rebuilt? There is a view that a brand new school will be built somewhere within the catchment area of Lepton and Kirkheaton. Others would prefer the School to be rebuilt on its present site. Whatever the decision, it is bound to cause controversy and upset. Let's hope that common sense prevails.

The success of King James's School over the years is down to the dedication of the staff

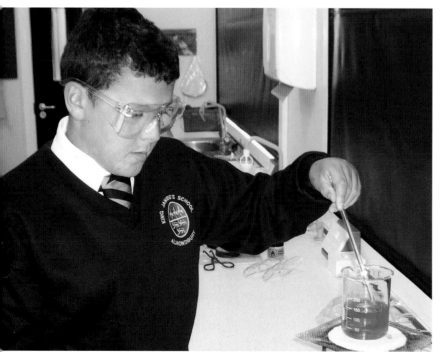

Rapt concentration: the School's designation as a Specialist Science College has been an important element in its success in recent years

who have worked here. Many of these staff have given long years of service to the School. Some have spent the vast majority of their career, if not all of it, working at the School. They make the school a great place to work at and a wonderful place to be educated. The longest serving member of the teaching staff is currently Patrick O'Brien who joined the School in September 1972. Patrick started as a Teacher of Classics and has seen many changes during his time at King James's School. He has had an extremely successful career, working in a variety of roles which culminated with his appointment as Deputy Headteacher in January 2004. Other staff who have worked at the School for over 15 years include Walter Raleigh, Lesley Rattigan, David Bradford, Angela Melling, Gillian Sykes, Carolyn Thirlwell, Ailsa Griffiths, Ian Gatenby, Kath Emerson and Ann Turner. They all follow the tradition of the many great teachers who have served King James's School so well.

There are also many long serving members of the non teaching staff. Lesley Walker, the Canteen Superviser, joined the school in October 1971. Everyone who has been at King James School since her arrival will know

Happy Birthday to us: King James's School students mark out the 400th anniversary of the Charter on the all-weather pitch

Lesley. She has a great love of the School and will not tolerate anyone saying anything remotely negative about it. Other long serving members of staff include Denise Porter and Nicole Green.

As we approach the 400th Anniversary of being granted the Royal Charter we look to the future with great optimism. We are a popular and successful school. Ofsted in January 2007 stated 'King James's School is an improving and inclusive school where standards are rising quickly.' We receive great support from our parents, the King James's School Foundation and the Old Almondburians. The financial help from the Foundation is invaluable as our funding still continues to be one of the worst in Kirklees. Their support allows us to purchase resources and equipment that enhances our educational provision. Thanks to them our students can benefit from the use of the latest equipment which helps to contribute to their understanding, development and progress. We have a strong and dedicated Governing Body who challenge and support us.

We have one aim – to become the best school in Kirklees. A school, that all our students, both past and present, are proud of. I firmly believe that in the very near future we shall achieve this aim. ◢

KEY

Current area usage, in the format, 'Ground floor/first floor' is shown in WHITE. In the case of the older parts of the School, many Old Almondburians will be more familiar with earlier usages shown, in the same format, in *YELLOW*.

1. Year 11 Common Room *Dining Room ('Wooden Hut')*

2. Reception/offices *Old Kitchen*

3. ODH/Reprographics *ODH/Dorm 4*

4. Schoolhouse *Schoolhouse*

5. ILC, offices/Staff Room *'Small'/Dorms 2 & 3*

6. Library *Library ('Big')*

7. Fenay Porch *Fenay Porch*

8. Classroom/Classroom *Junior lab/Dorm 1*

9. Classroom/Pastoral Base *Cloakroom/Art Room*

10. Science labs/Classrooms (Special Needs Dept on third floor) *Science labs/N1; N2; N3*

11. Portakabin classrooms (temporary)

12. Former grass tennis courts

13. Remains of 'Big Tree'

14. Science lab

15. Entrance; classroom *Entrance; Woodwork room*

16. Science labs *Hall and Gymnasium*

17. Geography classroom

18. Sports Hall

19. Music Room

20. Gymnasium and Drama Studio

21. Offices and languages classroom *Biology laboratory*

22. Dining Room

23. Kitchen

24. Design block (Computer room in central area)

25. Teaching block; computer rooms on first floor

26. Rugby field

Not shown: 'All-weather' sports pitch; football fields; cricket field

The buildings — then and now

ROGER DOWLING returns to King James's to discover how much — or how little — has changed over the years. He finds a fascinating mixture of old and new

The Schoolhouse (late C17th - 1760)

UNDOUBTEDLY the oldest part of the School, the Schoolhouse was the residence of the Master right up the time of Taylor Dyson's retirement in 1945. Alas, it does not date back to 1608: its pitched and sprocketed stone slate roof and mullioned windows suggest that the original house on the site was substantially rebuilt around 1760, and this is confirmed by the writings of Rev Samuel Brook, the Master at that time. However, some parts of the earlier buildings may well have been re-used: the distinguished architectural historian Sir Nikolaus Pevsner (1902-83) has expressed the view that the mullioned windows date back as far as 'late 17th century.' It is a Grade II listed building.

Like any old building, the Schoolhouse has needed constant repairs over the years. In 1868 a spectacular storm, as a result of which water rushed 'like a torrent' down St Helen's Gate, caused major damage to the Schoolhouse roof and the School received a portion of the £5,000 relief funding granted to the village for emergency repairs.

In the harsh Almondbury winter, the Schoolhouse could be a cold and cheerless place, with burst pipes and peeling walls. One of Taylor Dyson's early achievements was to introduce central heating into the School and Schoolhouse in 1915-16, followed by electric lighting in 1923.

Downstairs, the house

(Below top): The Schoolhouse around 1890 at the time of Rev Francis Marshall. It remained the Master's personal residence up to 1945: note the carefully tended lawns and borders
(Bottom): The same scene today. The exterior of the house (a Grade II listed building) has changed little over the years

Roger Dowling started his education at Moldgreen County School in 1946 and joined Almondbury Grammar School in 1952. He subsequently studied electrical engineering and electronics for four years at the Royal Radar Establishment College of Electronics in Malvern before joining the BBC. During the following 25 years, he worked variously in London, Leeds, Bristol and Manchester, where in due course he became head of engineering and programme services. Roger left the BBC in the late 1980s and became a director of a business support organisation. In 2000, he became a founding member of a business conference company. Now retired, he lives in Lymm, Cheshire. Roger is webmaster of the Old Almondburians' Society website and a member of the OAS Executive Committee.

1994: Clive Watkins reports on dry rot in the schoolhouse

'SEVERAL OUTBREAKS OF DRY ROT have been found in the oldest part of the School in the past few months. One appeared in my own room in the back corner opposite the door – that is, behind the large glass-fronted cupboard referred to above. It was a very small outbreak. More extensive was the wet rot which had destroyed the floorboards along the foot of the back wall and the wall parallel to the library. All this has now been put right.

'The plaster was stripped off, revealing for the first time in very many years the inner face of the stone from which the house is built. A damp-proof course was created by the injection of a sealant. The floorboards were replaced to a distance of eighteen inches from the wall and new skirting board was inserted to match the original. The damaged walls have now been re-plastered, a white anaglypta wallpaper has been put up throughout and the exposed timbers have been re-painted.

'The dry rot in my room was quite limited. Much more extensive was the outbreak found at the top of the stairwell above and behind my room. This had invaded Pat Reid's office (immediately above my own) and almost destroyed one of the main timbers running across her ceiling and supporting the roof. It had also bridged the head of the stairs and invaded the timber in the roof of the ODH at its end towards St. Helen's Gate, where the front wall of the upper storey abuts on to the rear wall of the original schoolhouse.

'When the workmen climbed up into this space, they were alarmed to find that the Victorian building had not been keyed into the older one: it was simply resting against it. This, together with the weakening of the structure caused by the dry rot, made them – very sensibly – down tools at once. Eventually it was decided to shore up the top of the building with steel jacks from below and that, with this protection, work could continue. The result was that for about a month I shared my room with three of these jacks while a further three were stationed outside my door supporting the stairwell.'

Clive Watkins gets his study back to himself

(Top): The living room of the Schoolhouse in the days of Robert Crump
(Bottom): The same scene today. Over 100 years later, Mrs Crump's fireplace is still in place; the room, for many years the secretary's office, is now the office of the Headteacher's PA

comprises what used to be a living room (later to become the school secretary's office and today the PA's office) and a parlour (still in use today, as it has been for many years, as the Headmaster's study). It was always a challenge to make the house into a comfortable home; the Crump family in particular made valiant efforts in this regard by installing in the early 1900s a fine new fireplace which is still in position today. Mrs Crump also acquired a Welsh dresser and various pieces of antique furniture in character with the house.

A curiosity of the Schoolhouse is that the low wooden ceiling beams in the living room and the parlour differ markedly, the former being quite plain and the latter being decoratively carved as befits a room which was

(Left, top and bottom): The wooden ceiling beams in the present PA's office are markedly plainer than those in the Head Teacher's study (bottom)

(Right): The fading Huddersfield Corporation coat of arms on the wall of the Head Teacher's study

traditionally retained for use on 'special'occasions. Moreover, the sets of beams run at right angles to each other (those in the living room running across its width and those in the parlour running along its length), indicating beyond doubt that the two rooms date from different periods.

An interesting discovery was made some years ago in the Headmaster's study when the walls were prepared for redecoration. Over the mantelpiece could just be seen the outlines of the Huddersfield coat of arms, no doubt dating back to the 1920s when Huddersfield Corporation took over responsibility for the School.

The former bedrooms on the first floor have been used for many purposes over the years. The School's first tiny biology laboratory was located here for several years until a purpose-designed laboratory became available as part of the 1955 extensions. Today the upstairs rooms are used for offices.

The Schoolroom and dormitory (1848)

THE ORIGINAL SCHOOL-ROOM, erected around 1755 at the time of Samuel Brook, was a single storey building located on the site now occupied by the ODH (except that it also extended across the corridor that now separates the ODH from the Schoolhouse). When Rev Alfred Easther arrived in 1848, it was on the clear understanding that he would be given a free hand in the School's future development, and he convinced the Governors that the way forward lay in the provision of accommodation for boarders so that the School could attract pupils from further afield.

Accordingly, work commenced later that year on a new schoolroom on the site of the old, but this time it took the form of a two storey building providing

This famous snowballing photograph dates back to around 1865. Behind the Schoolhouse can be seen the new schoolroom with dormitory above. The figure in the top hat is Alfred Easther. The building works of 1880/3 make it impossible to replicate this view today.

a dormitory (later to be known as the 'Old Dormitory and later still as 'Dorm 4') for the boarders above. The opportunity was also taken to make some improvements to the Schoolhouse so as to provide additional sleeping and living accommodation.

The far wall of the ODH bears a memorial to Rev Alfred Easther, and the Latin inscription translates:

Sacred to the memory of Rev Alfred Easther, Master of Arts, of Emmunuel College, Cambridge, who presided over this Royal School for twenty-nine years. He fell asleep in Christ on the 25th September in the year of our salvation 1876; a guardian of real culture, and a teacher of useful literature and branches of knowledge. Mindful not only of his example but also of his precepts, and feeling his loss, his pupils whom he attached to him by his affection, and whom he uplifted by his spotless character, have caused this marble table to be set up to him whose loss they mourn, in the year of our salvation 1880. Speaking the truth in love.
Ephes. iv. chap., verse 15

Although recognisably the same room, the ODH has changed significantly since the photograph on the left was taken in the early 1900s. The gas lights have given way to modern electrical fitments (electricity was installed in 1923), the fireplace on the far wall has been boarded over and the wallpapered walls and ceiling now glisten with paint. However, the 1880 memorial to Alfred Easther (below) remains in position on the far wall. On its left is the stained glass window Easther put in at his own expense in 1859

A new school entrance was also constructed, with a handsome external porch that still remains. The architect and surveyor for the work was Richard Armitage, himself an old boy of the School, and his contractor was Walter Capper & Jenkinson.

The new building cost £250 – a crippling sum in those days – but Nettleton's Charity came to the rescue with a generous grant of £200.

When the 'Big' schoolroom was built in 1883, the old schoolroom took on a new lease of life as a dining hall, eventually acquiring the name 'The Old Dining Hall' or 'ODH' that it has retained to the present day.

(Right): The old school entrance in 1916, and the same view today. A quaint structure, it was to suffer the indignity of becoming a boilerhouse when central heating was installed at a cost of £162 4s 6d [£162.22] in 1915/16: note the ventilation louvres inserted above the window

The kitchens and servants' quarters (1880)

BY THE 1870s, the policy of attracting boarders to the School was working well; so well, in fact, that the voracious appetites of the young boarders were placing the domestic catering facilities under considerable strain. Accordingly, the eminent Halifax architect

(Below left): The main school entrance in 1910, with the new kitchen block shrouded by trees behind, and the same view today. (Below right): The scene is much the same, except that one of the stone pillars has at some stage been removed and the attractive wooden gates have sadly gone. The carved stone above the high window on the gable end (inset) confirms the 1880 date of the building

William Swinden Barber was commissioned to design a new two-storey building in matching stone to adjoin the north wall of the Schoolhouse, and the Governors' Minute Book records that on 11th December 1880 'the new buildings were inspected and approved.'

On the ground floor, the new building provided a large kitchen; above were servants' quarters. In more recent times, with the disappearance of the boarders, the accommodation has been used for a variety of purposes: in the 1950s, the kitchens even housed the school tuckshop, and the music room was for many years located above. Today, the ground floor has become the school reception, whilst the upstairs rooms are used for offices and other ancillary functions.

The 'New classroom' and 'New dormitory' (1880)

THE ARCHITECTURAL PRACTICE of William Swinden Barber was under some pressure in the late 1870s for while the architect was busy designing the new kitchen block he was also hard at work preparing plans for new classroom and dormitories on the site, the extent of which the School had never before seen in its long history. The first stage, completed at the same time as the kitchen extension in 1880, took the form of a detached two storey stone building some 30 yards [27 m] from the south wall of the Schoolroom.

This provided a large new classroom downstairs, and a 'new dormitory' (better known later as 'Dorm 1') and master's bedroom above. The whole scheme was conceived by the Brooke family, with encouragement and financial assistance from the Governors and the Earl of Dartmouth. The 1980 buildings cost a total of £500: a major investment at the time but one which the School, with 21 boarders by 1980 and 36 a year later, clearly regarded as vital.

The new classroom was used for science teaching and

(Right): The former Science Lecture Room or 'Junior Lab' became a cloakroom for some years but is now again in use as 'Room 7'

(Far right): Dorm 1 today is also still a classroom today, known as 'Room 20'

became known as the Science Lecture Room and later as the 'New Lab'. In more recent years, Old Almondburians will remember it as the 'Junior Lab'; for some years it was demoted to become a cloakroom but it is pleasing to record that it is now once again in service as a general classroom.

Dorm 1 became a classroom after the departure of the boarders, acquiring an additional door in 1938/39 which provided a convenient connection with the corridor and classrooms (formerly N1, N2 and N3) adjacent. Dorm 1 is still in use for teaching today, currently as a mathematics classroom.

Three buildings that are no more: the Cloisters, the 1900 labs and 'the monstrosity'

The Cloisters (1868) is a building from the past of which no trace, alas, now remains. It was a detached building located just behind the Schoolhouse.

Its origins lie in a meeting, attended by Rev Alfred Easther, Rev L Jones (vicar of Almondbury) and a number of others, held at the School on 12th December 1851. The meeting resolved unanimously that those attending should form the committee of a society to cultivate chemical science to be known as 'The Chemical Society of King James's Free School in Almondbury.'

The objective of the Society was to stimulate interest in chemistry at the School and it was soon realised that a suitable laboratory and chemistry classroom was required. A fund-raising bazaar, held in 1860, raised £100 and by 1868 this had been boosted to some £160 through private subscriptions – enough to erect a detached building just behind the Schoolhouse on the site preciously occupied by Walter Smith's covered playground, the 'Cloisters', whose name it thereby inherited. It was one of the first such laboratories in the country, and for some years, under George Jarmain (described as 'the outstanding chemistry teacher in the north') the School enjoyed major successes in this important new subject. But after the departure of Jarmain and Easther in 1876 the 'Cloisters' became increasingly used as a general class room for senior boys and later as a small gymnasium. By 1900 it was virtually a ruin and in 1918 it was converted into an outside cloakroom. The 'Cloisters' was finally demolished in 1938 as a prelude to the major extensions that commenced later that year. It was a sad end to a pioneering little building.

For all his perceived failings as Master, Leonard Griffiths soon recognised when he arrived in 1897 that the School needed better science facilities. George Jarmain and his successors had achieved miracles in the Cloisters but proper science laboratories were now an urgent requirement.

And so, in 1900, a block comprising two laboratories was built adjoining the 'new' science lecture room that had been completed seven years earlier. Its location was roughly on the site now occupied by the two-storey buildings erected in 1938/9. The architect for the new laboratories was Mr John Haigh of Messrs Abbey and Hanson, and the contractors were Messrs Graham and Jessop. The building work itself cost £598 9s 4d [£598.46] and a further £242 12s 11d [£242.65] was spent in fitting it out with the latest scientific facilities.

Across the other side of the yard (shown here in 1937 with 'Big Tree' in the foreground) was the ugly brick-built Art and Woodwork building ('a monstrosity' according to Taylor Dyson) erected at haste in 1901. Its building had been a condition of a grant from the Board of Education when the School ceaased to be fully independent in that year. The building's demise in 1938 received general approbation.

Fenay Quad and the 1883 extensions

FENAY QUAD was formed in 1883 as part of the second stage of W S Barber's expansion plans for the School. To mark the occasion, a memorial stone over the new School entrance was laid by Mrs Blanche Brooke, wife of the President Governor and benefactor John Arthur Brooke; inscribed in Latin, the translation reads:

Unto the glory of the Father, Son and Holy Spirit, Blanche Brooke of Fenay laid the foundation stone of this school on the 2nd of August 1883.

By this date, the number of pupils at the School under Francis Marshall had risen to 76, and it was a time of confidence for the future. (Ironically, the confidence was not, in the event, fulfilled: numbers started to fall almost immediately and were down to 11 by 1897).

The scope of this phase of the work was truly ambitious. On the ground floor it provided a magnificent new schoolroom, named admiringly the 'Big' (later to become the Library), a smaller classroom

(Above): A large and distinguished assembly gathered for the unveiling of the foundation stone by 'Blanche Brooke de Fenay' on 2nd August 1883. (Top right): The 'new' School entrance around 1890, not long after it had come into service.

(Bottom right): Apart from a remarkably unsympathetic replacement of the ground floor window on the left (a process which, curiously, seems to have been reversed in the case of the window above), little has changed over the past 100 years

(known not surprisingly as the 'Small'), a locker room and a masters' common room. Above, it provided a further dormitory (the 'middle dormitory', later known as Dorms 2 and 3).

It was an expensive project. The original estimate was £1,650, of which £1,000 was generated through the sale of consols (government securities), the balance coming from accumulations of surplus income. In the tradition that continues to this day, the actual cost when the bill

(Above): Today, the wall between Dorm 2 and Dorm 3 has been removed, restoring the area to its original 'middle dormitary' condition. It now functions as the Staff Room, once again – at least after an excessively heavy lunch – providing welcome sleeping accommodation

(Left, top and bottom): To this day, the 'Big' – or the 'Library', depending on when one attended the School – retains the quiet elegance that it must have had when delivered by the proud architect and builders 125 years ago

arrived from the builder revealed an overspend of over 40%, bring the total cost up to £2,349 12s 6d [£2,349.62]. In the event, the overspend was put down to 'improvements not contemplated in the order' (another tradition that continues to this day), and the balance was covered by private subscription.

The contractors for the building work were Messrs B Graham and Nephew of Moldgreen.

The major extensions of 1938/9

THERE WERE 56 BOYS at King James's when Taylor Dyson arrived in January 1913. When control of the School passed to Huddersfield Corporation in 1922, the number had risen to some 250. The School was bursting at the seams.

Various interim changes were made to contain the situation. With the departure of the boarders, 'Dorm 1' became a classroom and the middle dormitory was partitioned to form what became known as classrooms 'Dorm 2' and 'Dorm 3'. The 'old dormitory' above the ODH also became a classroom, known subse-

quently as 'Dorm 4'. Four further classrooms were rented temporarily from the trustees of the Wesleyan Sunday Schools in the village. In 1924, the long covered

(Right): Edward Akroyd's drawing of the new entrance. Note the names of the four School houses stylistically commemorated in the stonework

was 'goodbye' to the 1900 laboratories, the Cloisters and the unlamented cheaply-built Art and Woodwork Room of 1901.

The new extensions provided large physics and chemistry laboratories, roughly on the site of the 1900 laboratories, a large cloakroom and toilet area, and a woodwork room. On the first floor were two general purpose class-rooms (somewhat unimaginatively known as N1 and N2, the 'N' standing for 'new'), a geography room (N3), a large staff room, and, to the rear, a superb well-light art room. There was also a purpose-designed new ground floor gymnasium/hall with adjacent showers, linked to the other new buildings by a corridor which also included a handsome new entrance.

It was a substantial project and the cost of over £17,000 was no insubstantial sum in those days. The buildings are still in use today, albeit in some cases performing different functions under different names. All the ground floor areas apart from the cloakroom now function as part of the School's science department whilst the upstairs rooms have been retained as general classrooms. In recent years, the provision of roof lights has made it possible to build yet further classrooms into the roof space. The gymnasium itself has been converted into further laboratories, with a preparation room at first floor level.

shed along the back of the School was converted into a dining room to accommodate up to 120 pupils at a sitting.

Surprisingly, it was not until the start of 1938 that a start was finally made to enlarge the School properly. The extensions of 1938/9 would effectively double its size, but not before some demolition had taken place. It

The later extensions

THE EDUCATION ACT OF 1944 laid down such lavish standards for school premises that there were real doubts in the late 1940s about whether King James's, with its limited premises and facilities, could survive. Fortunately, good sense prevailed and it was realised that the standards prescribed were excessively extravagant; this, together with the purchase of addi-tional land around the School, enabled King James's once again to face the future with confidence.

The first step, in 1955, was to establish a corridor, alongside the old woodwork room, leading on the left to

an impressive new Biology Laboratory (for some years, the only biology facilities had been in a tiny room above the headmaster's study) and a much larger staff room to accommodate the larger teaching staff. The project cost some £10,000.

Then, with financial and practical assistance from the Old Almondburians' Society, a new cricket pavilion was opened in 1958 to coincide with the 350th anniversary celebrations, replacing the old 'wooden hut' that had existed since Francis Marshall's time.

But this was only a start. A study by the Huddersfield

The new hall/gymnasium opened in 1963. An adjoining purpose-designed stage made it possible to use the area flexibly for drama productions, but later pressures on space eventually made it necessary to convert the stage into yet another teaching area.

Education Committee in 1959 identified numerous other respects in which the School's facilities were markedly deficient:

- No dedicated assembly hall
- Inadequate gymnasium
- Poor dining accommodation and no kitchen
- Still insufficient provision for science
- Deficiency of two classrooms
- A need for further library accommodation
- Shortage of wash-basins
- Far too little hard playing area
- Insufficient tennis courts

The outcome was that a massive £50,000 building programme was undertaken, culminating on 10th May 1963 with the grand opening of a new range of buildings adjoining the new biology laboratory and staff room. This provided the School with a 2,000 square foot [180 m²] gymnasium (still doubling as an assembly hall); an adjoining stage area for drama productions and recitals; a 1,700 square foot [153 m²] dining room; and a 1,200 square foot [108 m²] 'linking area' which could be used to extend either the gymnasium/hall or dining room. The changes to the old gymnasium mentioned earlier, to convert it into a laboratory, were also made at this time; also, the old detached dining room was converted into classrooms for music and languages. In due course, new hard tennis courts were also provided.

The 1979/80 extensions

The continued growth of the School together with its change of status from Grammar School to Sixth Form College and then to Comprehensive made further extensions essential in the late 1970s. Shepherd Building Group were on site by 1979 to commence work on an ambitious scheme that would provide:

- a 6,000 square foot [540 m²] Design Block
- a 2,000 square foot [180 m²] two storey Teaching block
- a magnificent 5,000 square foot [450 m²] Sports Hall.

The Design Block provided the School for the first time with dedicated areas for teaching textiles, metalwork, woodwork and home economics.

The Sports Hall was a welcome addition to the School's indoor sports facilities. Sport has always been taken very seriously at King James's: inset is the trophy cabinet

Likewise, in the Sports Hall, the School at last had a dedicated hall for sports training; it is interesting to note that the 'new' gymnasium of which Taylor Dyson was so proud in 1938/9 could be accommodated three times over in this vast new building.

The 2002 Laboratory and the Music Room

The most recent extensions are a new laboratory for the School's expanding Science Department and a Music Room, both erected in 2002 to a virtually identical exterior design.

Located at the rear of the site adjacent to the gymnasium and drama studio, the Music Room provides the School with its first-ever purpose designed music classroom, appropriate in a town which has always been renowned for its fine music-making tradition.

The new laboratory is located in the school yard adjacent to what used to be the showers and changing room for the 1938/9 gymnasium/hall and virtually on the site of the School's well-loved former 'Big Tree.' Appropriately, it takes King James's into the 21st century: a fine array of solar panels was mounted on the roof in 2006 and helps to cut carbon dioxide – and reduce the School's electricity bills. ▼

They made it into the public eye

King James's has produced many prominent figures over the years. ROGER DOWLING nominates a few for his personal 'King James's School Hall of Fame'

KING JAMES'S has always been a relatively small school and it is a testimony to its values over the years that so many of its former pupils have gone on to enjoy successful careers all over the world. Limitations of space preclude a mention of more than a handful; but here we salute just a few Old Almondburians whose activities, over the past century or so, have thrust them into the public eye.

We begin just over 100 years ago with the eminent actor **SIR FELIX AYLMER** , who was actually a boarder at the

School for three years from 1897 under Leonard Griffiths as Master. His full name was Felix Aylmer Jones and he had a supporting role in many films and television plays between 1933 and 1968, usually playing a doddery judge, a bureaucrat or (perhaps recalling his schooldays) a schoolteacher. He starred in just one film: *Mr Emmanuel* (1944) in which he took the title role playing the part of an elderly European Jew living in Manchester. Felix Aylmer was knighted in 1965 and died in 1979.

Another future knight of the realm was **HAROLD HIMSWORTH** who attended King James's for several years from 1916 and went on to become Secretary of the Medical Research Council. A research scientist of the highest calibre (a specialist on diabetes), he received honours from many universities and was knighted in

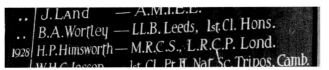

1952. The following year he was appointed Honorary Physician to the Queen. Sir Harold died in 1993.

One of Harold Himsworth's contemporaries was **BENJAMIN WORTLEY**, who entered King James's in 1918. After graduating at the University of Leeds, he had a brilliant legal career and in due course became Professor of Jurisprudence and International Law at the University of Manchester. He played a prominent role in discussions with the Ministry of Education in 1948 when

the future of King James's as a grammar school was in serious doubt.

In more recent times, the name of **STEPHEN COWARD** (1948-1957) has also become prominent in the field of Law. A leading criminal silk, he regularly prosecuted or defended in cases of fraud, murder and other serious crime. His high profile cases included defending the assistant bosun of the *Herald of Free Enterprise* which capsized in Zeebrugge harbour in 1987, and defending Ian Huntley in the Soham murder trial of 2003. Stephen Coward also has extensive experience of medical issues and acted for the prosecution in the case of Deborah Winzar, the nurse jailed in 2000 for the murder of her husband by injecting him with insulin.

DAVID MORPHET (1951-58), Head Boy at the time of the 350th anniversary, went on to achieve a Double First in English at Cambridge. In 1961 he joined HM Diplomatic Service, serving in the Middle East and Madrid and in the Foreign Secretary's private office. Transferring in 1974 to the Department of Energy, he later became UK Governor at the

Aeneas meanwhile climbed the cliff ...

AENEAS meanwhile climbed the cliff, and scanned
The whole, wide, wind-swept sea, far out from land.
He looked for Antheus' ship with troubled eye:
Capys and Laicus he could not descry.
There was no ship in sight. But on the shore
Three noble wandering stags, with many more
Were pasturing through the valley down below.
He started—snatched his arrows and his bow
Which good Achates had been carrying.
The proud and haughty leaders he did fling
Unto the ground and then with arms he drove
The common herd among a leafy grove.
And as seven ships were lost the day before
Seven stags, as tribute now lay on the shore.
The harbour reached he thence; amongst all shared
The wine from Sicily's shore, all unimpaired
By death, as were its drinkers, who were calmed
By Aeneas' words, from fears of comrades harmed.
'My friends (for you've known evil times before),
You've heard the Scyllan horror that doth fling
His rocks. Restore your hopes now undermined
By anxious fear—perhaps to call to mind
E'en this will be pleasant in future days.
Latium approaches slowly through a haze
Whereby the kind Fates will once more give us peace
From irksome troubles, and our labours cease.
There shall great Priam's Kingdom rise again:
Endure, prepare for future without pain.'

*Carefully coached by Jim Toomey, David Morphet (3 alpha) won
the Latin Verse Speaking Competition (a set piece from Virgil's
Aeneid) at Leeds University in 1954. Afterwards, he translated it
for The Almondburian.*

Moving to the world of sport, the name of **DEREK IBBOTSON** (1942 - 1949) (right) will live on as the finest athlete produced – so far – by King James's. He entered the School in 1943 and soon revealed his sporting ability. Ibbotson ran his first sub four minute mile in 1956 at the White City (3 mins 59.4 secs) and later the same year won the bronze medal in the Melbourne Olympic Games when he achieved a time of 13 mins 54.0 secs in the 5,000m final. His illustrious running career produced many other fine performances, which included a 3 mins 58.5 secs mile (the second-fastest ever recorded at the time) to mark the birth of his daughter Christine in June 1957. A month later he set up a new World Record of 3 mins 57.2 secs at the White City, against a field of the world's greatest runners. Today, he lives – in retirement but still enjoying his sport – in Ossett, West Yorkshire.

Another fine sportsman produced by King James's is **JEFFREY NEILSON TAYLOR** (below) who attended the School from 1940 to 1947 and became an amateur soccer player with Huddersfield Town while still at school in 1943. He gained a BA (Hons) degree in Geography/Geology at University College, London, funding his studies by turning professional with Huddersfield Town in a debut match against Chelsea. As he was studying in London, he welcomed the opportunity in due course to transfer to Fulham in 1952. He then spent three years with Brentford before retiring from football in 1958.

International Atomic Energy Agency in Vienna at the time of the Chernobyl disaster in 1986. In 1989 he moved to the private sector and was Board Member of London's largest power station, Barking Power Ltd, and Director-General of the post-privatisation Railway Forum (1997-2001). David was a founder member of the national charity *Rethink* (formerly National Schizophrenia Fellowship), and was its Chairman from 1977-82. His various publi-cations over the past six or seven years have included a full-length biography of the Victorian journalist and MP Louis Jennings; five collections of poetry (to be found at www.notionbooks.co.uk); and a book *St John's College Cambridge - Excellence and Diversity* published in 2007.

● *David Morphet's brother Alan was at King James's from 1956 to 1963, and subsequently read English at Oxford. Sadly, he died in 2002.*

to studies at the Royal College of Art in London where, by a happy coincidence, a new musical group calling themselves 'The Temperance Seven' found themselves short of a banjo player and enlisted John to fill the vacancy. Within a couple of years, The Temperance Seven hit the jackpot when their recording of *You're Driving Me Crazy* shot to the top of the UK hit parade, closely followed by *Pasadena*. Today, John is still a busy banjo player and entertainer with his group 'Bill Posters Will Be Band', offering 'a complete musical variety show suitable for a wide range of functions', and he also continues his graphic design activities. He now lives in Teddington, Middlesex.

But this was only the start of a new career in the public eye. Having become deeply involved in music making while at university, Jeff spent five years studying at the Royal Academy of Music in parallel with his footballing activities. His retirement from football presented the opportunity to embark on a successful career as the baritone Neilson Taylor, making many radio and television broadcasts, appearing at Glyndebourne with the Glyndebourne Opera Company and at Covent Garden. In 1974, he was appointed Professor of Singing at the Royal Scottish Academy of Music and Drama whilst continuing as a top performer on radio and television. Jeff retired from RSAMD in 1992 but, now living in Holmfirth, continues to teach privately at the highest level.

Music of a different kind was to prove the basis of a successful career for **JOHN WATSON** (1948 - 1953) (below). Even in his schooldays, John Watson was an entertainer: one of his earliest memories is making a papier-mâché set of Punch and Judy figures which in due course led to a Christmas show in the School gym. Sadly, his voice broke before he could realise his ambition to appear in a Gilbert and Sullivan production and after five years he left King James's to pursue his interest in Graphic Design. This led

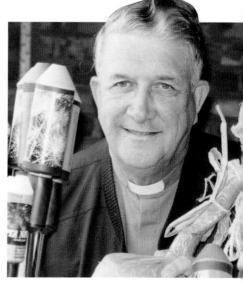

Theology and pyrotechnics make an unusual mix, one might think. But **REV RONALD LANCASTER MBE** (1942 - 1950) (right) thought otherwise and now has become renowned as the School's 'Master Blaster Pastor.' He is the founding owner of *Kimbolton Fireworks*, the UK's market leader in firework production and operator-fired displays. Fascinated by fireworks and chemistry from his very early years growing up in Huddersfield, the historical centre of the UK fireworks industry, his interest in Chemistry was further aroused at School by Dr Calloway and Ron began experimenting with pyrotechnic devices. In due course, he helped to organise displays for the local community during the Second World War, at a time when fireworks were not available. In later years Ron was appointed as Chaplain and taught chemistry at Kimbolton School in Cambridgeshire where his passion for fireworks grew, and he carried out extensive research for the firework industry from his newly constructed workshops. As the reputation of the Reverend Lancaster's fireworks and displays grew, *Kimbolton Fireworks Ltd* was formed in 1964.

In 1956, a King James's schoolboy by the name of **GORDON KAYE** (1952 - 1959) made his reluctant

stage debut as Lord Scroop, Earl of Masham in Frank Anderson's production of Henry V. Although this also marked the end of his school acting career (even now, he shudders at thoughts of his 'performance'), he became an amateur actor with Bradford Amateur Theatre group before joining Bolton Rep at the newly formed Bolton Octagon as a professional earning £18 a week. A year later he was spotted by Patricia Phoenix ('Elsie Tanner' in Coronation Street) which led to appearances as Elsie Tanner's nephew, accompanied by a welcome tenfold increase in his weekly remuneration. This led to an invitation to play the part of cafe owner René Artois in a projected new BBC comedy series set in Nazi-occupied France during the war. It became so popular that some 90 episodes were eventually recorded and are still repeated regularly today. The show also led to a massively successful London and internationally touring stage show. This, and other stage appearances all over the country, result in Gorden (the slight and involuntary change of name occurred as a result of a typing error when he joined the actors' union *Equity*) remaining a very busy actor today. He now lives in Leeds.

The writer **MICHAEL HARDCASTLE MBE** (above right) attended King James's from 1944 to 1951. A prolific writer of children's books, mainly on a sporting theme, he received the MBE in 1988 for his services to children's literature. On leaving school, he spent five years in the Royal Army Educational Corps serving in the UK, Kenya and Mauritius, before joining *The Huddersfield Examiner* as a reporter in 1956. He subsequently worked on the *Bristol Evening Post* as a diarist and

literary editor, and moved to the Liverpool Daily Post as chief feature writer in 1965. Michael Hardcastle's first book *Soccer is Also a Game* was published in 1966 to coincide with the World Cup. Since then he has written 147 more books, mainly about sport, on such topics as cricket, motocross, horse-racing and tennis. He made a generous donation to the School library in 1994 and was guest speaker at Speech Day that year.

Another eminent writer, who sadly died in August 2007, was **MICHAEL JACKSON** (below) who left King James's at the age of 16 in 1958 to become a trainee on the *Huddersfield Examiner*. He had already submitted news stories and jazz reviews and soon became a successful and highly distinctive reporter.

He moved to Fleet Street where it was a natural progression in those days to develop a healthy interest in beer. This was further stimulated by the Campaign for Real Ale launched in the 1970s and in 1976 Michael Jackson brought out his first book *The English Pub*. The

following year, he wrote his *World Guide to Beer* which brought him fame in the United States and many other parts of the world. His deep interest in Belgian beers led to *The Great Beers of Belgium* (1991) which has been published in 18 languages and has sold over three million copies. Such was the gratitude of the country's brewing industry that Crown Prince Philippe of Belgium gave Jackson the Mercurius Award for services to Belgian beermakers.

In 1989 he published *Michael Jackson's Malt Whisky Companion* – the world's best-selling book on the subject – followed in 2001 by *Scotland and its Whiskies*.

Michael Jackson was a huge draw as a lecturer on beer and sometimes had crowds of 1,000 or more – though he modestly claimed that many must have come by mistake, expecting his pop-star namesake.

BRYAN HOPKINSON (1967-1974), former British Ambassador to Bosnia, left King James's and university with a desire to travel but without the cash. A career in the Diplomatic Service proved an ideal solution, leading

to postings to Kampala and Lisbon, followed by an appointment as Ambassador in Sarajevo in 1995 where he oversaw Bosnia's transition from war to peace. He then decided to pursue a freelance career, working initially for the International Crisis Group, a non-governmental organisation working to prevent and resolve deadly conflict around the world. For them he established an office in Kosovo immediately after the NATO bombings of 1999 – a time of lawlessness, where revenge in the form of arson and murder went unpunished. In 2000, he moved to Montenegro and recently he worked again in a calmer Kosovo as a member of the UN administration.

Bryan Hopkinson has now returned to the UK, living currently in Huddersfield. Nostalgically recalling school cross-country runs, he has now developed an enthusiasm for long-distance walking.

I return to the sporting theme for the final entry to my King James's School Hall of Fame. The cricketer **RYAN SIDEBOTTOM** (above) attended King James's from 1989 to 1994. Son of the famous cricketer and footballer Arnie Sidebottom, Ryan made his county debut for Yorkshire as a left-arm seamer in 1997. In 2000 he was the leading English-qualified bowler in the domestic averages, earning his county cap in the process, and won a nomination for the Cricket Writers' Club Young Cricketer of the Year. In 2001, he made his England debut, briefly replacing the injured Matthew Hoggard in the first Test against Pakistan. Ryan left Yorkshire in 2004 to enjoy new success with Nottinghamshire where, in 2005, he took 50 first-class wickets to become the Player of the Year and help Nottinghamshire to win the Championship for the first time in 18 years. He made a highly successful return to the English test side in 2007. ◢

A picture is worth a thousand words

This drawing by Peter Meal shows the 'new' physics and chemistry labs and, on the right, 'Big Tree' in all its glory in the late 1930s

The old cricket pavilion, drawn above by Roger Sykes, dated back to Marshall's day. Roger Dowling's drawing shows its 1958 replacement

The former grass tennis courts, with Fenay Porch and the Library, are shown in this 1950s pen and ink drawing by Brian Littlewood

This recent artistic view of the Old Kitchen entrance yard today is an acrylic by Jack Denbigh-White

This drawing by Roger Sykes shows the corridor between the Head's Study and the ODH. Note the ancient desk on the left, still preserved today

The School's picturesque buildings have long been the inspiration for drawings and paintings by pupils and staff. They provide a fascinating pictorial account of the School's growth over the years

Haymaking in the field behind the School? An unbroken view of Almondbury Church from the old Art Room? These 1950s drawings by Roger Sykes show how dramatically the School has grown in recent years

Art Master Edward Akroyd was very keen on scraper board drawings and encouraged his pupils to try their hand at the technique. His view of the former Schoolroom entrance shows the old wooden dining room on the right

Fifty years separate these views of the Old Kitchen entrance, both by Brian Littlewood. In the 1950s he drew the attractive scraper board drawing shown above. When more recently he painted the fine acrylic below, he counted the number of windows in the kitchen with particular care

The School seen from Farnley Line. Scraper board drawing by Gavin Kane

Tailpiece: voices from the past

What is left from our schooldays apart from memories, asks GERALD HINCHLIFFE. He finds answers in the writings of three notable Old Almondburians

AS YOU PERHAPS sigh with relief that this wander through four centuries of our School's history is drawing to a close, you may hear or have heard many voices from the past. Those of your schoolday companions; those of masters and Almondburians from across the world. Many have recorded their memories for posterity on the Old Almondburians' website; other reminiscences you may have heard across a crowded bar.

May I recall three of those voices? The distinguished actor and former boarder Felix Aylmer spoke at a London Old Almondburians' Society dinner in the 1960s and recalled visiting the School in 1931. Taylor Dyson met him at the station and drove him at high speed to Almondbury village. Once there he asked if he might walk down St Helen's Gate. It was a summer's day. There was not a soul in sight; and a great stillness hung over everything. He said he had an uncanny feeling of being young again. He passed the house where his friend, Hallas, used to live. Then, there it was – the School. Nothing seemingly had changed. He roamed familiar places – the Big, the ODH and the Small. Then he opened the door to Dorm 4 where he had lived all those years ago. No stage set could have been more evocative. He recalled:

I have travelled the world. But nowhere else have I had such a sense of belonging.

Some time ago, a 93-year-old gentleman, one William Braide, wrote to the School expressing his desire to be present at the major celebrations in 2008. 'Bill' was a master at the School from 1936-39, leaving to serve in the RAF throughout the Second World War. Thereafter he had a distinguished career in education, becoming an administrator with overall control of all London's schools.

In his recollections, Bill wrote with great warmth and pleasure of his days at Almondbury. Recalling the happy days he spent with his very first form, he concluded:

They were an exceedingly bright and responsive bunch and my happy relationship with them contributed more than a little to making my three years at AGS the happiest of all my 40-year career in education.

When, as the years roll on, we only half remember Ohm's Law, the Romans, photosynthesis, and the square on the hypotenuse, what is left from our schooldays? What lingers after our days at King James's? One would like to think through all the experiences of school we will have developed a mature sense of what it is to be a human being. Tolerance, personal responsibility, social awareness and a sense of service are values which have hopefully emerged from the School's traditions and way of life.

The third voice, that of Victor Emsley, sums it up succinctly. Victor, a sixth-former in 1953, was to have a short life, yet one of great literary promise. Meditating on the vivid experiences of life, he concluded with these lines:

These bright drops in the lifepool
Make the struggle worthwhile
Justifying our eternal fight for worthiness.

Our ancestors at King James's School sought over four centuries to 'make the struggle worthwhile'; our descendants, we hope, will continue the 'eternal fight for worthiness.' ◾

Floreat Schola Almondburiensis

The ever-changing world of education policies in England

EDWARD ROYLE asks what education is for and charts the national events and ideas that have influenced changes in educational thinking over the years

The provision of education in the West has, throughout most of its history, been seen as a work of charity; that is, an aspect of religious activity, a 'good' performed freely for the benefit of the next generation. In England until the later nineteenth century, schools offering an education above the most elementary level were usually provided, controlled and staffed by the Church and financed through the charitable giving of the living and the bequests of the dead. Though the form and content of education has changed with society and politics over the centuries, at the heart of educational activity from the chantry school of late-medieval England to the Founders' Day service of more recent times, there has been a remarkable continuity. But over the past two hundred or so years the pace of social, political and economic change has quickened, challenging the accepted values and expectations of each generation until over the lifetimes of most Old Almondburians change has become so rapid as to be qualitative rather than merely quantitative.

Few politicians would dare affirm to-day, what Enoch Powell was still prepared to assert in the 1970s, that education was a charitable activity. Now schools are having to demonstrate to the Charity Commissioners what their charitable activities are; to be merely educating the next generation is no longer enough.

What is education?

This begs the question, 'What is 'education'?', which invites a further question, 'Is it the same as training?' The latter is certainly necessary. Each generation needs to pass on to its successor the skills as well as values necessary for survival and in no economy can this be ignored. But such a view assumes little or no social mobility: each son or daughter is to replicate his or her father or mother; and it assumes that the skills of one generation will continue to be relevant to the next.

For centuries before the great economic and social changes at the end of the eighteenth century that we call 'the industrial revolution', this was accepted. Girls in particular could be taught the necessary skills at home; boys could be apprenticed into another family. Only a few needed to be trained for higher things. A celibate clergy had to recruit the next generation from among the children of the laity and so schools were founded to prepare bright boys, often from relatively poor homes, for the priesthood. The educational ladder was invented to serve the Church which in turn provided the personnel to staff the institutions of state. On the bottom rung a local priest might conduct lessons in basic vernacular literacy as a side activity to saying prayers for the dead of his sponsors. The ablest pupils would be taught Latin, the language of the medieval Church. The very brightest might aspire to

Edward Royle benefited from King James's historic charter in that he came to the school from Linthwaite township in the ancient parish of Almondbury as a foundation scholar in 1955. He went on to Cambridge to read history in 1962, remaining there to complete his PhD in 1968 and then to become a fellow of Selwyn College. In 1972 he moved to the history department at York where he remained until retirement in 2004, having risen through the ranks from lecturer to professor, serving time along the way as head of department. He is now Emeritus Professor at York. He has published widely on the social and religious history of Britain since the eighteenth century, with a special interest in the local history of Yorkshire.

enter the colleges of Oxford and Cambridge, which were in effect seminaries for the Church; such boys would require sponsorship and so this phenomenon has been termed 'sponsored mobility', carefully controlled so as to reinforce rather than challenge the existing social order.

Renaissance and Reformation

Almondburians like to think that their school is special - as indeed it is for them. But the historically interesting thing about the school is that it is completely typical, exemplifying at almost every point in its history what was happening to scores of local schools throughout the country. It began as a chantry school which was then transformed by two great intellectual forces: the Renaissance and the Reformation. First, the Renaissance opened up for the elite in society a different view of education. In the Middle Ages even the higher degrees of the universities had been functional in that they had prepared boys for certain professions - the Church, the Law and Medicine.

Now the idea developed that education was worth having for its own sake, for its cultivation of the mind. Latin, to which Greek was added, opened up the culture of past civilisations as well as a better understanding of the Bible. Such an education was not tied to the servile condition of mere utility; it was liberal, freeing the spirit of those who could employ others to do mundane service for them. And this appealed to the lay gentry, who were beginning to take an interest in schools and universities beyond the immediate concerns of the Church. Indeed this is sometimes seen to be one of the reasons why the laity challenged the Church and why the Reformation took the course that it did.

By the time the Tudors were on the throne of England, the country had in Henry VIII and his children - son and daughters - the most highly educated monarchs the country had hitherto known. The same was true throughout Europe: in Scotland James IV set the trend for the house of Stuart, so when Elizabeth was succeeded on the throne of England by James VI and I in 1603 the Court continued to set a fashion for education that was copied by aristocrats and gentry alike across the land.

So it can be no cause for surprise that, following the Reformation and the dissolution of the chantries in 1547 which imperilled the beginnings of education in local areas, it was the neighbourhood gentry who showed concern and sought to revive these schools, making education now their 'core business'. The support given to the St Helen's school by the Kaye family of Woodsome was but one example of a common feature of educational provision in the later sixteenth century. To gain status and some kind of legal identity, royal charters were sought and 'King Edward VI' and 'Queen Elizabeth' schools appeared across the country. In York, there was even a foundation in the name of King Philip [of Spain] and Queen Mary. The gentry of Almondbury were rather slow in not getting in their request for royal favour until the reign of King James, a tardiness they appear to have shared with the good folk of Knaresborough.

Such schools were to teach 'grammar' - that is, Latin and, in some cases, Greek, in preparation for university entrance. And they were to do so freely to children of the parish, which in the case of Almondbury stretched far to the west to include the chapelries of Honley, Meltham and Marsden. Not all children would have gone on to university, but some would: the bright sons of clergymen (for the clergy could now marry) and others aspiring to enter what Reformation zeal demanded should be a graduate clergy; and the more easy-going sons of the gentry wanting a smattering of liberal education without necessarily taking a degree before spending a little time at the Inns of Court in London to fit them for their duties as local landowners and magistrates.

The schoolmaster was invariably - and was sometimes required to be - a graduate and thus would have been at least a clergyman in deacon's orders, perhaps a badly paid curate from some local church who needed the little extra income that could be made from teaching the pupils subjects other than grammar (which was free). This purpose of preparation for university entrance necessarily kept the grammar schools small, but local demand and the need to provide foundation literacy in the vernacular led some masters to start a 'petty school' to which in some cases it appears even girls were admitted.

The teacher might be a member of the master's family, a respectable dame of the parish, or a boy from the grammar school before going on to university or after leaving there and in search of his first curacy. The latter sort might also work in the grammar school itself as an assistant or 'usher' if numbers warranted it and finances permitted.

Classics or Charity?

The course of education provision is frequently determined by fashion, and the fashion among the gentry for a liberal education in grammar schools followed by university lasted over a hundred and fifty years; but by the later seventeenth century it was played out. The schools were still needed for boys aspiring to be clergymen but Oxford and Cambridge were no longer seen as finishing schools for the gentry: numbers at the universities fell along with their reputations; grammar schools felt the impact.

Charity found new outlets in promoting the basic skills of the poor: reading, religion and, perhaps writing for boys and more likely sewing for girls. With rare exceptions the poor did not want a free education in Latin grammar. The dilemma of the eighteenth century grammar schools was Classics or Charity? Should they provide a classical education free of charge to that minority, largely the gentry, who could afford to pay, whilst charging the poor for English subjects? Or should they forfeit their grammar school status and become charity schools to provide a free - or, more usually, subsidised - education for the poor?

Different schools provided different answers. In some growing centres of population there was still sufficient demand for a traditional grammar school with parents prepared to pay to have their sons educated alongside a few poor scholars 'on the foundation'. At that greatest of all chantry foundations, Eton, where the aristocracy sent their sons, only one per cent of pupils in the second half of the eighteenth century were poor boys. Some grammar schools benefited from their locations. As London grew more crowded and unhealthy, the attractions of Harrow on the uplands north of the metropolis proved appealing. But little could protect schools from parental perceptions of irrelevance. In Bristol, which had a hundred pupils in the mid-eighteenth century, there were none at the start of the nineteenth. Even Manchester saw a fall in admissions.

Schools in market towns and rural areas suffered most. At Pocklington in the East Riding the schoolmaster was absent and the schoolroom was let for a sawpit! Whether such places survived depended to a great extent on their endowments. Land values were rising in the later eighteenth century, so a school with a good endowment invested in land could be doing well financially even if no parents wished to send their sons to it to receive what they perceived to be an irrelevant classical education. Other schools were less fortunate in their endowments and investments. When Clitheroe Grammar School received from Queen Mary the proceeds of the tithes of Almondbury parish in the 1550s it did well; King James had no such bounty to bestow on the Grammar School at Almondbury in 1608. Perhaps this was the penalty for a late start?

The challenge of the industrial revolution

Parents who wanted their local schools to become more relevant were dealt a severe blow in 1805 in a case involving Leeds Grammar School. The wealthier citizens wished to turn their grammar school into a commercial school for the middle classes, teaching French rather than Latin, but the Lord Chancellor ruled that 'grammar' meant the learned languages - that is, Latin and Greek - so endowments could be used to promote only this purpose.

Not until 1840 were grammar schools allowed to develop their curricula freed from the more restrictive requirements of their foundations. This allowed some schools to concentrate on the classics and the middle classes. Where such schools were well situated on the new railway network they could build national reputations, as at Rugby. Other schools were able to respond to local demands to develop commercially.

The losers were invariably the poor, but by the early nineteenth century these were being catered for by a new surge in the provision of charitable schools, largely attached to the Church of England under the auspices of the National Society for Promoting the Education of the Poor in the Principles of the Established Church (founded 1811 and with state aid from 1833). Small grammar schools struggled to find a niche among these competing demands and rival institutions. Under the guidance of able masters, some survived but many did not.

The means by which Almondbury survived are detailed by Gerald Hinchcliffe elsewhere in this publication. The mid-nineteenth century was a great era of educational enquiry and reform as the state responded to changing attitudes towards ancient privileges and restrictions and to new demands from the economy for an education appropriate to the new age of industry and commerce. The Newcastle Commission (1861) enquired into the provision of elementary education; the Clarendon Commission (1864) enquired into the nine 'great' public schools; and the Taunton Commission (1868) reported on the 791 endowed schools in between, including the one at Almondbury.

This report led to a recasting of some endowments, so that some foundations were split, with a little money going to set up schools for girls - hence those implausibly-named King Edward VI and Queen Elizabeth schools for girls. Above all, grammar schools were now allowed to use their endowments to develop a new function as commercial schools for the middle classes alongside their older task of preparing a few boys in the classics for university entrance.

This was, though, a crowded market, for while the grammar schools had been hamstrung by their outdated statutes, companies of proprietors had set up commercial schools to meet modern needs. The schools inspector and son of the famous headmaster of Rugby, Matthew Arnold, had called for what he termed 'a French Eton', meaning Eton-like schools devised to provide a liberal but cheaper education for the Nonconformist middle classes whom he feared were like uncivilised 'Philistines'; but in a northern industrial town with numerous Nonconformist manufacturers interested in passing their skills and values on to the next generation, it was more important to set up proprietary schools on a joint stock basis, made in their own image, than to support an ancient grammar school identified with the Church of England, offering the prestigious but irrelevant classical subjects often from a secluded rural location miles away from the centre of activity.

Almondbury was fortunate in that, although two new proprietary schools were established, the Anglican Huddersfield Collegiate and its Nonconformist rival, Huddersfield College, financial difficulties and religious rivalries prevented them becoming a real threat, the two eventually combining and then closing in 1893.

New competition

Of more significance for the smaller grammar schools was the development of local authority education under increasing regulation from the central state. Initially this concerned elementary education only and was channelled through school boards elected by local rate-payers under an Act of 1870, but these boards soon aspired to teach subjects beyond the elements of reading, writing and arithmetic.

By the 1890s many urban areas also had what were termed Higher Grade Schools as well as separately-funded Technical Schools. Huddersfield had both; and though at first only two of the 470 pupils in the Higher Grade School were from Almondbury, the market place was becoming crowded. The Bryce Commission on Secondary Education (1895) concluded its review of Almondbury with some foreboding: 'It is difficult to see what its future place will be ... it would certainly suffer by the founding of a good secondary school in Huddersfield.'

This is what followed after 1902 when a dispute over whether school board funds could be used for non-elementary education was resolved by transferring responsibility for the provision of secondary education to committees of local councils. Most towns had acquired borough status with their own elected councils during the course of the nineteenth century (Huddersfield in 1868); and all counties were governed by elected local councils from 1889. The instruments and legislative powers were now in place for a complete restructuring of secondary education in the twentieth century.

Education after 1902

The competition effectively ended the existence of many small grammar schools. The larger ones or those with large endowments survived but smaller ones such as the grammar schools at Longwood (founded 1731) and Fartown (founded 1770) disappeared in 1920 and 1928 respectively. New local education authority schools took their place or took them over.

Huddersfield College was re-opened as a Municipal Secondary School in 1909. In 1904 it was made possible for existing schools to be supported financially from the rates and this threw them a lifeline, though with financial aid came a loss of independence: one condition was the admittance of a quarter of pupils from local elementary schools, and another was representation of the local authority on the governing body. Whereas in 1904 there were fewer than five hundred grant-aided secondary schools, by the First World War there were over a thousand. In 1919 secondary schools without independent financial means were given the choice of accepting a direct grant from the Board of Education or of accepting grant-aid from their local education authorities. The majority chose the latter course, and this is what the governors of Almondbury did in 1922.

Schools thus financed were now subject to the twin constraints of local and national control. Locally this was exercised through the governing body of the school; nationally by central government policy. An Education Act in 1918 raised the school-leaving age to fourteen, but this is when the majority of pupils then left. Only a minority proceeded to secondary school around the age of eleven or twelve - perhaps fifty-six out of every thousand, and most of these left after completing the new Secondary School Certificate, an examination administered by the universities which in effect fixed the curriculum of secondary schools in the old grammar-school mode.

Very few took the Higher School Certificate and proceeded to university, although a small number of state and local authority scholarships were now available and the range of universities had greatly expanded beyond Oxford and Cambridge to include London and, by the later nineteenth century, provincial centres like Leeds and Sheffield. The problems of the national economy in the 1920s and 1930s, though, meant that these decades were better noted for their reports on education than for actual developments.

The new world after 1944

This situation changed after the Second World War. The Education Act (1944) finally broke down the boundaries between elementary and secondary education. Now all children were to pass from the primary stage to the secondary stage, although a national test locally administered at the age of eleven would determine the sort of secondary school to be attended by children. Those judged to have academic potential - about a fifth of the total - went to grammar school, though most still did not proceed to university. The School Certificate was replaced by examinations leading to a General Certificate in Education (GCE) at both Ordinary ('O') and Advanced ('A') levels in individual subjects. The former was usually sat at the age of sixteen but the age for compulsory schooling was

raised only to fifteen. Most grammar school pupils, though, remained to take their GCE 'O'-levels and increasing numbers stayed on for their 'A'-levels at eighteen. The creation of a new examination for the less able, the Certificate of Secondary Education (CSE) in 1963 and the raising of the school-leaving age to sixteen in 1973, had little relevance for most grammar schools.

The 1944 Act created a secondary education for all without specifying what form that should take. In theory grammar, technical and modern schools were to be provided to meet the needs of all aptitudes. In practice, technical schools were provided at the age of eleven only in the larger cities and the modern schools came to be regarded as where the 'eleven plus' failures went when they failed to get into grammar school.

Critics of this system held that to send pupils to different schools was socially divisive, and they also questioned the child psychologists on whose work the idea of academic selection at the age of eleven was based. The 1944 Act, though, also allowed for the transfer of all pupils at the age of eleven into a single, comprehensive school, and one of the first purpose-built comprehensive schools in the country (and the first in the county) was built by the West Riding in the Colne Valley at Linthwaite - once a far-flung corner of the parish of Almondbury - in 1956.

The provision of such schools became policy for the Labour Party, led by politicians many of whom had themselves climbed the slender ladder of opportunity from grammar schools to university. In 1964 Labour came to power, led by Harold Wilson, who had attended Royds Hall Grammar School, opened by the Huddersfield and West Riding Education Committees in 1919.

Nationally, pressure for change became almost irresistible. The primary argument was one of social engineering. The existing eleven-plus system did not offer equality of opportunity; it judged children prematurely and on false premises; it was socially divisive. There was also an educational argument. Thanks partly to the influence of Robert Morant, principal civil servant at the Board of Education after 1902, those grammar schools like Almondbury that survived to become grant-aided had modelled themselves on those which had evolved into 'public schools' in the nineteenth century, which in turn were modelled on the 'Clarendon nine'. So not only did they continue to offer a liberal education based on the classical curriculum but they also adopted other trappings from the public schools - notably the 'house' system, which had originated when boarding schools had adopted the device of housing their pupils at the school under the superintendence of a master instead of boarding them out in town; and the 'prefect' system, whereby the older boys were given special privileges in turn for helping keep the younger boys in order.

By the 1960s the grammar school curriculum was looking narrow and dated. It was inflexible and in the smaller grammar schools offered little choice of subjects, lacking especially those 'new' academic subjects in the social sciences (which were becoming 'university subjects' in the newer universities), as well as a wider range of languages spoken more often in business circles than classical Latin (Russian was in vogue). Harold Wilson's concerns for the state of the British economy and the lack of relevance in the tone and content of its elite educational provision drove him to call for a technological revolution.

Polytechnics (including one at Huddersfield) were started in 1968. Women were entering higher education and the professions in increasing numbers. The ancient purpose of grammar schools to prepare boys for Oxford and Cambridge, still less the Church, was looking distinctly dated. During the 1960s and 1970s the comprehensive revolution spread; it reached Huddersfield, and Almondbury, in 1973.

The perpetual revolution

Since that date the ever-increasing frenzy of politicians trying to meet the needs of social engineering, individual opportunity and the requirements of the national economy all at the same time has led to a plethora of reforms, 'initiatives', acts, directives and re-directives too numerous to be counted here. In another part of this publication Dave Bush has chronicled what it was like to be on the receiving end. In 1988 the GCE 'O'-level and CSE examinations were merged to create the GCSE and a 'National Curriculum' was established. Education policy entered the age of micro-management as, in the name of consistency, an attempt was made to impose uniformity across schools. The temptation for government to crowd the curriculum with topics and subjects deemed (for the moment) to be essential proved too great. Examinations multiplied and with them

performance 'League Tables'. The future of the GCE 'A'-level came under increasing scrutiny. In the 'Curriculum 2000' a new examination after one year of sixth-form studies (the 'AS'-level) was introduced alongside a requirement for students to specialise in more than three subjects after GCSE. (At Almondbury, students on the Arts side had once studied five subjects in 'Transitus' without benefit of any central instruction or examination.) Finance, fashion and flexibility meant that the 11 - 18 Comprehensive model (and the 'middle school' and 14 - 18 models) gave way in many towns to an 11- 16 model followed by a Sixth Form College, completing for good or ill the destruction of the grammar school as reconstructed by Robert Morant after 1902.

With the decline in Latin teaching, the introduction of subjects the academic value of which was (and is) much disputed, and the serious failure of schools at large to produce either adequate basic numeracy and literacy in one half of the population, or a desire to study science and technology in depth in the other, the questions, 'What is education for' and 'How should it be provided?' remain unanswered. It is no longer only for the elite (and only for boys); it is no longer a work of charity. The uncertainty that remains promises that another, much revised, edition of this publication will be needed well before King James's School celebrates its half millennium in 2108. ◢

WHO'S WHO IN 2008

TEACHING TEAMS

LEADERSHIP GROUP

Headteacher: Robert Lamb
Deputy Headteacher: Patrick O'Brien
Assistant Headteachers: Amanda Costello, Sean Kelly, Angela Melling, Walter Raleigh, Ian Rimmer
Advanced Skills Teachers: Jacqueline Armitage (English), Robert Handy (Science)

CURRICULUM TEAMS

ENGLISH
Stephen McNamara (Curriculum Team Leader), Zoe Brunning (Second), Jacqueline Armitage (Advanced Skills Teacher), Carrie Grassby, Robert Howell, Ann Jackson

HUMANITIES/PERSONAL SOCIAL HEALTH CITIZENSHIP EDUCATION/RELIGIOUS EDUCATION
Carolyn Thirlwell (Curriculum Team Leader), Kim Rutherford (Second), Elizabeth Atkinson, Amanda Costello, Lorraine Buckley, Rachel Holland, Sean Kelly, Ruth Pocock, Walter Raleigh, Melanie Tobin, Adam Wilkinson

MATHEMATICS
David Price (Curriculum Team Leader), Robert Travers (Second), John Britton, Kathryn Gouldin, Wayne Horn, Robert Lamb, Ian Rimmer

MODERN LANGUAGES (inc Classics/Latin)
Lesley Rattigan (Curriculum Team Leader), Naomi Pinkney (Second), Pascale Bradbury, Ailsa Griffiths, Patrick O'Brien

PERFORMING ARTS
Nick Fazakerley (Curriculum Team Leader), Kathryn Brooke-Benn

PHYSICAL EDUCATION
Anna Di Napoli (Curriculum Team Leader), Susan Birkett, Ian Gatenby

SCIENCE
Rebecca Walton (Curriculum Team Leader), William Butcher (Second), Steve Briggs, Beverley Dannatt Kath Emerson, Robert Handy (Advanced Skills Teacher), Rachel Taylor, Sarah Valovin

SPECIAL NEEDS
Sam Burns (Special Educational Needs Coordinator); Halina Dorrington

TECHNOLOGY
Ann Turner (Curriculum Team Leader), Kirsty Ambrick (Second), Angela Melling, Gillian Sykes, Maxine Turnell

INFORMATION AND COMMUNICATION TECHNOLOGY
Palwinder Kang (Curriculum Team Leader), Laura Curran

SUPPORT TEAMS

ADMINISTRATION
Head's PA/Administration Manager: Tracey Dean
Clerical Support Assistant: Nicole Green
Reprographics Officer/Clerical Support Assistant: Nicola Ramsden
Clerical Support Assistant: Val Wright

OPERATIONS OFFICER (Data Manager & Timetable)
David Bradford

PASTORAL
Behaviour & Attendance Manager: Sean Folan
P.A. to Behaviour & Attendance Manager and SENCO: Janette Button
Personal Assistant to Pastoral Leader: Sue Cope

FINANCE
Business Manager: Alison James
Finance Officer: Lesley Stead

ICT
Network Systems Manager: Alison Proud
ICT Technician: John Lea

INDEPENDENT LEARNING CENTRE
School Librarian: Jenny Ainger

CAREERS OFFICER
Susan Stead

TECHNICIANS
Science: Karen Jazwinksi
CDT: Daniel Booth
Assistant Science/CDT: Sarah Smith

LEARNING SUPPORT
Behaviour Support Workers: Yvonne Day, James Dickinson
Teaching Assistants: Amanda Simms, Joy Stainthorpe

LUNCHTIME SUPERVISORS
Senior Supervisor: Denise Porter
Supervisors: Andrea Feery, Carole Lloyd, Gillian Scott, Julie Thewlis, Lesley Walker (and Staffroom Attendant)

SITE STAFF
Caretaker: Keith Ramsden
Assistant Caretaker: Bob Farrell

KING JAMES'S GOVERNING BODY

Mr Robert Lamb (Headteacher)	Mr Andy Peaden
Mr Patrick O'Brien (Deputy Head)	Mr Brian Ruttle
Mrs Margaret Barrow	Mr Andrew Schofield
Mr Nich Briggs (Vice Chair)	Mrs Andrea Slater
Mr Richard Dean	Mr Brian Stahelin (Chair of Governors)
Ms Lesley Earnshaw	Mr Jack Taylor
Mr John Eastwood	Ms Vanessa Thomas
Mrs Samantha Eva	Mrs Sandra Todd
Mr Andrew Haigh	Mrs Rebecca Walton
Mr David Harling	Mr Chris Wise

PRIZES IN 2008

YEAR 7

The Doreen Hinchliffe Prizes for Highest Academic Achievement
Form Prizes for Progress and Effort
(sponsored by the 'Young' Old Almondburians' Society)

YEAR 8

Thorpe House Nursing Home Prizes for Highest Academic Achievement
Form Prizes for Progress and Effort
(sponsored by The Old Almondburians' Cricket Club)

YEAR 9

The Marsden Brothers Huddersfield Central Ltd Prizes for Highest Academic Achievement
Form Prizes for Progress and Effort

YEAR 10

The Dave Bush Prizes for Highest Academic Achievement
Form Prizes for Progress and Effort
(sponsored by The Old Almondburians' Badminton Club)

YEAR 11

Prizes awarded for performance in GCSE Examinations
The Jack Taylor Prizes for Highest Academic Achievement
Prizes for results – not the highest, but worthy of recognition
(sponsored by The Old Almondburians' Tennis Club)

- Austin Holroyd Prize for Deputy Head Girl
- Bill Chapman Cup for Lower School Maths
- Brooke Memorial Prize for English
- Burmah Star Shield for Design
- Cempak Trophy for Upper School Netball
- Crawshaw Prize for Cricket
- David Meal Memorial Prize and Caseau Cup for Modern Languages
- David Shires Prize for Design Technology
- David Taylor Memorial Prize for Sporting Achievement outside School
- Dobson Prize for Most Improved Boy Footballer
- Easther Cup for Local Studies
- Edwards Cup for Modern Languages
- EGL Abrasives Ltd Prize for Food Technology
- Francis Bareham Prize for History
- G & A G Douglas Prizes for Sportsmanship
- Gail Hall Cup for Lower School Netball
- Gorden Kaye Prize and Shield for Drama
- Governors' Prize for Sociology
- Graham Sellens Prize for Lower School Cross Country (Girls)
- Harry Taylor Prize for Classics/Latin
- House Shield for Sport
- Hudson Prize for Geography
- I Shaw Prize for Current Head Boy
- J M Shaw Prize for Current Head Girl
- Jack Boothroyd Memorial Prize for Biology

- King James's School Prize amd Morris Cup for Highest Academic Achievement
- KJS Prize for Humanities
- KPMG Prize for Deputy Head Boy
- Leslie Mallinson Memorial Prize for Chemistry
- Lyles Prize for Textiles Technology
- Martin Sellens Prize for Lower School Cross Country (Boys)
- Michael Hardcastle Prize and Trophy for Creative Writing
- Michelle Dodsworth Memorial Prize for Service to the School
- Morgan Prize for Music
- Napier Prize for Art
- Old Almondburians Chaplain's Prize for Religious Education
- Old Almondburians Jessop Prize for Mathematics
- Parent Link Group Prize for Attendance
- Parent Link Group Prize for Citizenship
- Prize for Performing Arts
- Rev Sam Herbert Memorial Prize for Progress and Effort in RE
- Richard & Nicole Green Prize for French Conversation
- Stafflex Prize for Games Captains
- Stephenson Shield for Public Speaking
- Sue Hacker Memorial Prize for Upper School Cross Country (Girls)
- Sue Hacker Memorial Prize for Upper School Cross Country (Boys)
- Syngenta Prize for Science
- Thomas Broadbent Prize for Physics

SCHOOL SONGS

The present School Song was a joint effort by 'Tich' Blackburn and Harry Gledhill, and was first performed at the 1936 School Pageant. Since then, no formal School occasion has been complete without a rousing rendition of this stirring composition:

Beloved School, to thee we raise
With joyful hearts our song of praise.
When e'er our thoughts to thee are turned,
We'll offer thanks for all we've learned.
> *Floreat Schola, Floreat Schola*
> *Floreat Schola, Almondburiensis!*

Here stood, as ancient records state,
A chantry school at St Helen's Gate.
For this our song of thanks we'll sing;
In praises loud our voices ring:
> *Floreat Schola, Almondburiensis!*

A charter granted by King James
Restored the School with loftier aims.
To him our gratitude is due,
For him our praises we'll renew:
> *Floreat Schola, Almondburiensis!*

O dearest School beneath whose shade
Our childhood games we oft have played,
Though from thy care we must depart,
We yet will sing with joyful heart:
> *Floreat Schola, Almondburiensis!*

Some Old Almondburians will remember with affection the previous 'off-the-shelf' School Song*, the words of which are given below†:

Hark! boys, hark! the early bell is calling,
Sweet and fresh, the morning air blows in:
Rise at once! the laggard is the loser;
All the work is moulded by the way that you begin.
> *Onward, upward, that's the golden Rule,*
> *Careful for the honour of the dear old School,*
> *Upward, onward ne'er let ardour cool,*
> *Ever strive for glory of the dear old School.*

Press boys press, the goal is hard to come by,
Dodge or wait, be ready for a run:
Pace needs breath, and breath will come by training,
Never take a beating 'til the game is fully won.
> *Onward, upward …*

Play up boys! and never heed the slogger,
Field or bowl as if you meant to win:
Play for side and not for self advantage,
Selfishness in cricket, as in life is real sin.
> *Onward, upward …*

On! boys, on! from Primer on to Caesar,
'Tout fin fait' be this your motto still
'Tout fin fait' with noble aims before you,
Do the work that's nearest, boys, and do it with a will.
> *Onward, upward …*

On! boys, on! when school is past and over,
Strive 'til death for God and for the Right,
Slow or quick, continue ever upward,
Truth and honour leading to the Day of Perfect Light.
> *Onward, upward…*

OUR DEAR OLD SCHOOL / Matthew Kingston (Novello and Company, 1905)
†*Our thanks to Austin Holroyd (1936-41)*

Subscribers

Nick Addy, Mirfield
Geoffrey Ainley, Almondbury
Ruth Ainley, Goole
David Anderson, Chislehurst
J Neville Armitage, Newark
Michael N Atkinson, Ulverston
Robert A Bailey, Marsh
Paul Balderstone, Almondbury
Melanie Barraclough, Amsterdam
M Barrow, Lepton
Jonathan Barstow, Chippenham
David Beach, Minehead
Robin Beaumont, Shefford
Godfrey Bedford, Honley
David Boothroyd, Cambridge
Gary Boothroyd, Richmond
P Bradbury, King James's School
Simon Brett, Ashton Keynes
N J Briggs, Almondbury
John Broadbent, Golcar
Neville Broadbent, Clare
Stephen Brooke, Wakefield
Michael Grover Brown, Thongsbridge
Norman Burluraux, Germany
P L Burns, Cirencester
Alan M J Bush, Longborough
Dave Bush, Porthcawl
E B Carter, Shepley
Trevor T Carter, Almondbury
D J Chambers, Freckleton
Colin Cheesbrough, Netherthong
J M Clarke, Sedbergh
Stephen Clarkson, Netherton
James Clayton, Old Catton
Graham Cliffe, Almondbury
Stephen Coward, Scaldwell
Keith Crawshaw, Almondbury
David G Croft, Almondbury
G Darby, Alwoodley
P D Davies, Lindley
Dr A E L Deeson, Faversham
Allan Dobson, Brighouse
Geoffrey Douglas, Shepley
Dr D J Dowling, Wokingham
Roger Dowling, Lymm
David B M Earles, New Mill
A C Earnshaw, Crosland Moor
D Earnshaw, Farndon
Lesley Earnshaw, Fenay Bridge
John Eastwood, Sowerby Bridge
Ronald Edwards, Frodsham
Andrew Firth, Grimsby
Dez Gay, Brentwood
Richard Geldard, Skelmanthorpe
Ian A Gelder, Swindon

Stephen A Gelder, Swindon
Neil Gledhill, Holmfirth
R Goldsmith, Scarborough
George Gothard, Jersey
Michael Green, Macclesfield
R J & N G Green, Netherthong
Andrew Haigh, Almondbury
I R Hales, Netherton
K R Hall, Sefton
Michael Hardcastle MBE, Beverley
Dr John A Hargreaves, Halifax
David Harpin, Huddersfield
Terence Haworth, Huddersfield
D Heptonstall, Matlock
David E Hinchliffe, Almondbury
Gerald Hinchliffe, Wollaton
David M Hirst, Leamington Spa
Garry L Hirst, Lindley
Austin Holroyd, Almondbury
Bryan Hopkinson, Huddersfield
Derek Ibbotson, Ossett
Andrew Ilchyshyn, Coventry
Mrs A James, Almondbury
Barry Johnson, Doncaster
D P Johnson, Kenilworth
Norman Kerrod, Brighouse
Sq Ldr Franciszek Kornicki, Findon Village
Michael & Thomas Ladlow, Dalton
Robert Lamb, King James's School
Rev R Lancaster MBE, Kimbolton
Paul Leadbeater, Shipston on Stour
Ken Leech, Australia
Geoffrey Lees, Edenthorpe
Brian Littlewood, Wistaston
Alan Lodge, St Albans
E M Lumb, Cowlersley
Christopher Makin, Mirfield
Mrs K M Makin, Mirfield
Tony Makin, Mirfield
Dr R F N Mallinson, Stourbridge
Roger Mallinson, London
Christopher Mann, Whitwell
S McNamara, King James's School
Dr David Mellor, West Bridgford
David H Mitchell, Horley
E D Mitchell, Longwood
Robert Moorhouse, Offerton
David Morphet, London
Michael Adrian Morris, Chapel Brampton
Nichola Mott, Northenden
Ian H Nesbitt, Bath
Helen Paton, Enfield
Richard Pearce, Huddersfield
David Pollard, Winchester
Michael Powner, Huddersfield

Walter Raleigh, King James's School
Pat Reid, Ilkley
J W Rennison, Tewkesbury
Peter Ridgway, Peebles
John Ridings, Wetherby
Tim Roberts, Shelley
Howard Robinson, Huddersfield
Colin Robson, Bath
C J Rockett, Haywards Heath
Rev Stuart W Roebuck, Newsome
Prof Edward Royle, York
Andrew Schofield, Kirkheaton
John Leonard Segar, Bishop's Stortford
Martin Sellens, Blackheath
J P Senior, Almondbury
F J Sheard, Almondbury
Richard G Sheard, Whitchurch
Alison Shelton, Jersey
Peter Smith, Mirfield
Brian Stahelin, Lepton
Gerald Stead, Lindley
Mrs L Stead, St James's School
J Stott, Almondbury
P J Summers, Kidderminster
Donald R Sykes, Burgess Hill
J A Sykes, Jackson Bridge
Rod Sykes, France
Andrew Taylor, Knowl Hill
Denis Taylor, Halifax
Jack Taylor, Halifax
Jeff Taylor, Scholes
Jonathan D Taylor, Almondbury
J R Taylor, Ossett
Gordon Teal, Adel
J S Thompson, Cheadle
David Tomlinson, Weeton
Dr J P Toomey, Stourport-on-Severn
Peter Tracey, Whitley Bay
Mrs A Turner, King James's School
P C Turner, Macclesfield
David Utley, Weston-super-Mare
William B Varley, Solihull
Richard P Wade, Almondbury
B D Wadsworth, Lepton
D R H Walker, Torquay
Ian Walker, Wakefield
P K Ward, Canada
John Watson, Teddington
Christopher Whiteley, Ross-on-Wye
Michael Wilkinson, Lancaster
Anthony Withers, Alvaston
Martin Wood, Bradford
Val Wright, King James's School
R C Young, Tibenham

INDEX

Note: Principle references are shown bold: **24**. *Illustrated references are shown in red:* 36